YOU
SHALL
KNOW
THE
TRUTH

YOU SHALL KNOW THE TRUTH

Sister Halima Hadiya

CITIOFBOOKS, INC.
3736 Eubank NE Suite A1
Albuquerque, NM 87111-3579
www.citiofbooks.com
Hotline: 1 (877) 389-2759
Fax: 1 (505) 930-7244

Ordering Information:
Quantity sales. Special discounts are available on quantity purchases by corporations, associations, and others. For details, contact the publisher at the address above.

Printed in the United States of America.

ISBN-13:   Softcover   979-8-89391-176-3
             eBook   979-8-89391-177-0

Library of Congress Control Number: 2024941167

No longer will you be called Abram; your name will be Abraham, for I have made you a father of many nations.

—Genesis 17:5

Then God said to Abraham, "As for you, you must keep my covenant, you and your descendants after you for the generations to come.

—Genesis 17:9

Understand, then, that those who believe are children of Abraham. The Scripture foresaw that God would justify the Gentiles by faith, and announced the gospel in advance to Abraham: All nations will be blessed through you. So those who have faith are blessed along with Abraham, the man of faith.

—Galatians 3:7–9

If you belong to Christ, then you are Abraham's seed, and heirs according to the promise.

—Galatians 3:29

And they sung a new song, saying, Thou art worthy to take the book, and to open the seals thereof: *for thou wast slain, and hast redeemed us to God by thy blood out of every kindred, and tongue, and people, and nation.*

(Revelation 5:9)

Men and brethren, children of the stock of Abraham, and whosoever among you feareth God, to you is the word of this salvation sent.

—Acts 13:26

Peace and Love

Contents

Acknowledgements

First of all giving thanks to our heavenly Father for his plan to send His son to save us, when we could not save ourselves and to the Holy Spirit for allowing us to remember the grace of God through studying Scripture. I must also give thanks and honor to the Lord Jesus Christ, (*whose name in Hebrew is* **Yahushua;** *meaning: Salvation*), for giving us the opportunity for everlasting life!

I would like to thank my only son, Marcus, for showing me by example that the Scripture (*Proverbs 22:6*) is true which states "train up a child in the way he should go and when he is old he will not depart."

For it does my heart good to know he is a child of the living God!

I would like to especially thank my loving husband Malcolm, for helping me with the Poems and Scriptures. For helping get this book done, knowing it was a strong desire of mine to get it out to our people. Because of his understanding of who we are (the children of the most high GOD), he made it his mission to help complete my mission. And I am forever grateful to him.

I would like to thank Elizabeth for giving me her time to help with the book. And to my brother Abdullah the founder of the Some One Cares Unity Center, for our many spiritual conversations. This book is truly for him.

Throughout life, we store information collected from experiences and try in some way to make sense of it. When we are not able to fully understand the things that occur in our lives, we often externalize the information. By doing this, we are afforded a different perspective, thus allowing us to think more clearly about difficult or perplexing events and emotions.

Poetry is one of the ways in which I choose to externalize my thoughts.

Poetry is a very powerful tool by which I can share sometimes confusing, sometimes perfectly clear concepts and feelings with others.

Before you begin **perusing** this **work**, and **if** you are a believer in the Lord Jesus Christ be sure you have named your sins privately to God the Father. **For** if we confess our [known] sins, He is faithful and righteous to forgive us our sins and to cleanse us from all unrighteousness [unknown, or forgotten sins]. *(1 John 1:9)*

You will then be in fellowship with God, filled with the Holy Spirit, and ready to learn doctrine from the Word of God.

"God is spirit, and those who worship Him must worship in [the filling of] the spirit and [biblical] truth." *(John 4:24)*

If you have never personally believed in the Lord Jesus Christ as your Savior, the issue isn't naming your sins. The issue is faith alone in Christ alone.

"He who believes in the Son has eternal life; but he who does not obey [the command to believe in] the Son shall not see life, but the wrath of God abides on him." *(John 3:36)*

THE WORD OF GOD is alive and powerful, sharper than any two-edged sword, piercing even to the dividing asunder of the soul and the spirit, and of the joints and the marrow, and is a critic of thoughts and intents of the heart. *(Heb. 4:12)*

All Scripture is God-breathed, and is profitable for doctrine, for reproof, for correction, for instruction in righteousness; that the man of God might be mature, thoroughly furnished unto all good works. *(2 Tim. 3:16-17)*

Study to show thyself approved unto God, a workman that needeth not to be ashamed, rightly dividing the word of truth. *(2 Tim. 2:15)*

Peace & Love

And I will put enmity between thee and the woman, and between thy seed and her seed; it shall bruise thy head, and thou shalt bruise his heel. —*Genesis 3:15*

1

Adam and Eve

THE PROMISE OF THE GREAT FIVE DAYS AND A HALF
(EXCERPTS FROM THE *FORGOTTEN BOOKS OF EDEN*)

But He was wounded for our transgressions, He was bruised for our iniquities:
the chastisement of our peace was upon Him;
and with His stripes we are healed.

—Isaiah 53:5

For God So Loved the World!
A poem by Sis. Halima

For God so loved the world
that He gave His only son
and whosoever believes in Him
He would save each and every one.
God knows that He's perfect
God knows that He's just.
He sent Him here upon this earth
to save every one of us.

He knew from the beginning.
they'll be some that will refuse
and the condemnation they will get
will only make them lose.
But for those of us who love Him.
We know from deep within
That the purpose of His coming
was to take away all sin.

If you have heard about the son
and do not understand.
Our Father sent Him to this world
to die for sinful man.
And now you have a choice to make.
it's something you must do.
For when Christ died to save us
He died especially for you.

For God so loved the world, that He gave His only Begotten Son,
that whosoever believeth in Him should not
perish, but have everlasting life.

—John 3:16

Lost Books of the Bible

Chapter III

Concerning the promise of the great five days and a half.

1. God said to Adam, "I have ordained on this earth days and years, and thou and thy seed shall dwell and walk in it, until the days and years are fulfilled; when I shall send the Word that created thee, and against which thou hast transgressed, the Word that made thee come out of the garden and that raised thee when thou wast fallen.

2. "Yea, the Word that will again save thee when the five days and a half are fulfilled."

3. But when Adam heard these words from God, and of the great five days and a half, he did not understand the meaning of them.

4. For Adam was thinking that there would be but five days and a half for him, to the end of the world.

5. And Adam wept, and prayed God to explain it to him.

6. Then God in His mercy for Adam, who was made after His own image and similitude, explained to him, that these were 5,000 and 500 years; and how *One* would then come and save him and his seed.

7. But God had before that made this covenant with our father, Adam, in the same terms, ere he came out of the garden, when he was by the tree whereof Eve took the fruit and gave it him to eat.

8. Inasmuch as when our father Adam came out of the garden, he passed by that tree, and saw how God had then changed the appearance of it into another form, and how it withered.

9. And as Adam went to it he feared, trembled and fell down; but God in His mercy lifted him up, and then made this covenant with him.

10. And, again, when Adam was by the gate of the garden, and saw the cherub with a sword of flashing fire in his hand, and the cherub grew angry and frowned at him, both Adam and Eve became afraid of him, and thought he meant to put them to death. So they fell on their faces, and trembled with fear.

11. But he had pity on them, and showed them mercy; and turning from them went up to heaven, and prayed unto the Lord, and said:

12. "Lord, Thou didst send me to watch at the gate of the garden, with a sword of fire.

13. "But when Thy servants, Adam and Eve, saw me, they fell on their faces, and were as dead. O my Lord, what shall we do to Thy servants?"

14. Then God had pity on them, and showed them mercy, and sent His Angel to keep the garden.

15. And the Word of the Lord came unto Adam and Eve, and raised them up.

16. And the Lord said to Adam, "I told thee that at the end of five days and a half, I will send my Word and save thee.

17. "Strengthen thy heart, therefore, and abide in the Cave of Treasures, of which I have before spoken to thee."

18. And when Adam heard this Word from God, he was comforted with that which God had told him. For He had told him how He would save him.

Chapter XIV

The earliest prophecy of the coming of Christ.

Then Adam said unto God: "O Lord, take Thou my soul, and let me not see this gloom anymore; or remove me to some place where there is no darkness."

2. But God the Lord said to Adam, "Verily I say unto thee, this darkness will pass from thee, every day I have deter-

mined for thee, until the fulfillment of My covenant; when I will save thee and bring thee back again into the garden, into the abode of light thou longest for, wherein is no darkness. I will bring thee, to it—in the kingdom of heaven."

3. Again said God unto Adam, "All this misery that thou hast been made to take upon thee because of thy transgression, will not free thee from the hand of Satan, and will not save thee.

4. "But I will. When I shall come down from heaven, and shall become flesh of thy seed and take upon Me the infirmity from which thou sufferest, then the darkness that came upon thee in this cave shall come upon Me in the grave, when I am in the flesh of thy seed.

5. "And I, who am without years, shall be subject to the reckoning of years, of times, of months, and of days, and I shall be reckoned as one of the sons of men, in order to save thee."

6. And God ceased to commune with Adam.

Chapter XV

1. Then Adam and Eve wept and sorrowed by reason of God's word to them, that they should not return to the garden until the fulfillment of the days decreed upon them; but mostly because God had told them that He should suffer for their salvation.

Chapter XXI

Adam and Eve attempt suicide.

1. Then Adam and Eve went in search of the garden.

2. And the heat beat like a flame on their faces; and they sweated from the heat, and wept before the Lord.

3. But the place where they wept was nigh unto a high mountain, facing the western gate of the garden.

4. Then Adam threw himself down from the top of that mountain; his face was torn and his flesh was flayed; much blood flowed from him, and he was nigh unto death.

5. Meanwhile Eve remained standing on the mountain weeping over him, thus lying

6. And she said, "I wish not to live after him; for all that he did to himself was through me."

7. Then she threw herself after him; and was torn and scotched by stones; and remained lying as dead.

8. But the merciful God, who looks upon His creatures, looked upon Adam and Eve as they lay dead, and He sent His Word unto them, and raised them.

9. And said to Adam, "O Adam, all this misery which thou hast wrought upon thyself, will not avail against My rule, neither will it alter the *covenant of the 5,500 years.*

Chapter XXIV

A vivid prophecy of the life and death of Christ

1. Then the merciful God, good and lover of men, looked upon Adam and Eve, and upon their blood, which they had held up as an offering unto Him; without an order from Him for so doing. But He wondered at them; and accepted their offerings.

2. And God sent from His presence a bright fire, that consumed their offering.

3. He smelt the sweet savour of their offering, and showed them mercy.

4. Then came the Word of God to Adam, and said unto him, "O Adam, as thou hast shed thy blood, so will I shed My own blood when I become flesh of thy seed; and as thou didst die, O Adam, so also will I die. And as thou didst build an altar, so also will I make for thee an altar on the earth; and as thou didst offer thy blood upon it, so also will I offer My blood upon an altar on the earth.

5. "And as thou didst sue for forgiveness through that blood, so also will I make My blood forgiveness of sins, and blot out transgressions in it.

6. "And now, behold, I have accepted thy offering, O Adam, but the days of the covenant, wherein I have bound thee, are not fulfilled. When they are fulfilled, then will I bring thee back into the garden.

7. "Now, therefore, strengthen thy heart; and when sorrow comes upon thee, make Me an offering, and I will be favourable to thee."

Chapter XXVI

A beautiful prophecy of eternal life and joy the fall of night.

1. Then Adam took Eve, and they began to return to the Cave of Treasures where they dwelt. But when they neared it and saw it from afar, heavy sorrow fell upon Adam and Eve when they looked at it.

2. Then Adam said to Eve, "When we were on the mountain we were comforted by the Word of God that conversed with us; and the light that came from the east, shone over us.

3. "But now the Word of God is hidden from us; and the light that shone over us is so changed as to disappear, and let darkness and sorrow come upon us.

4. "And we are forced to enter this cave which is like a prison, wherein darkness covers us, so that we are parted from each other; and thou canst not see me, neither can I see thee."

5. When Adam had said these words, they wept and spread their hands before God; for they were full of sorrow.

6. And they entreated God to bring the sun to them, to shine on them, so that darkness return not upon them, and they come not again under this covering of rock. And they wished to die rather than see the darkness.

7. Then God looked upon Adam and Eve and upon their great sorrow, and upon all they had done with a fervent

heart, on account of all the trouble they were in, instead of their former well-being, and on account of all the misery that came upon them in a strange land.

8. Therefore God was not wroth with them; nor impatient with them; but He was long suffering and forbearing towards them, as towards the children He had created.

9. Then came the Word of God to Adam, and said unto him, "Adam, as for the sun, if I were to take it and bring it to thee, days, hours, years and months would all come to naught, and the covenant I have made with thee, would never be fulfilled.

10. "But thou shouldest then be turned and left in a long plague, and no salvation would be left to thee forever.

11. "Yea, rather, bear long and calm thy soul while thou abidest night and day; until the fulfillment of the days, and the time of My covenant is come.

12. "Then shall I come and save thee, O Adam, for I do not wish that thou be afflicted.

13. "And when I look at all the good things in which thou didst live, and why thou camest out of them, then would I willingly show thee mercy.

14. "But I cannot alter the covenant that has gone out of My mouth; else would I have brought thee back into the garden.

15. "When, however, the covenant is fulfilled, then shall I show thee and thy seed mercy, and bring thee into a land of gladness, where there is neither sorrow nor suffering; but abiding joy and gladness, and light that never fails, and praises that never cease; and a beautiful garden that shall never pass away."

16. And God said again unto Adam, "Be long-suffering and enter the cave, for the darkness, of which thou wast afraid, shall only be twelve hours long; and when ended, light shall arise."

17. Then when Adam heard these words from God, he and Eve worshipped before Him, and their hearts were comforted.

They returned into the cave after their custom, while tears flowed from their eyes, sorrow and wailing came from their hearts, and they wished their soul would leave their body.

18. And Adam and Eve stood praying, until the darkness of night came upon them, and Adam was hid from Eve, and she from him.

19. And they remained standing in prayer.

Who Is He?
Nicodemus

Chapter XXII

1. After these things Pilate went to the temple of the Jews, and called together all the rulers and scribes, and doctors of the law, and went with them into a chapel of the temple.

2. And commanding that all the gates should be shut, said to them, "I have heard that ye have a certain large book in this temple; I desire you therefore, that it may be brought before me".

3. And when the great book, carried by four ministers of the temple, and adorned with gold and precious stones, was brought, Pilate said to them all, I adjure you by the God of your Fathers, who made and commanded this temple to be built, that ye conceal not the truth from me.

4. Ye know all the things which are written in that book; tell me therefore now, if ye in the Scriptures have found anything of that Jesus whom ye crucified, and at what time of the world he ought to have come: shew it me.

5. Then having sworn Annas and Caiaphas, they commanded all the rest who were with them to go out of the chapel.

6. And they shut the gates of the temple and of the chapel, and said to Pilate, Thou hast made us to swear, O judge, by the building of this temple, to declare to thee that which is true and right.

7. After we had crucified Jesus, not knowing that he was the Son of God, but supposing he wrought his miracles by some magical arts, we summoned a large assembly in this temple.

8. And when we were deliberating among one another about the miracles which Jesus had wrought, we found many witnesses of our own country, who declared that they had seen him alive after his death, and that they heard him discoursing with his disciples, and saw him ascending unto the height of the heavens, and entering into them;

9. And we saw two witnesses, whose bodies Jesus raised from the dead, who told us of many strange things which Jesus did among the dead, of which we have a written account in our hands.

10. And it is our custom annually to open this holy book before an assembly, and to search there for the counsel of God.

11. And we found in the first of the seventy books, where Michael the archangel is speaking to the third son of Adam the first man, an account that after five thousand five hundred years Christ the most beloved Son of God was come on earth,

12. And we further considered that perhaps he was the very God of Israel who spoke to Moses: "Thou shalt make the ark of the testimony; two cubits and a half shall be the length thereof, and a cubit and a half the breadth thereof, and a cubit and a half the height thereof."

13. By these five cubits and a half for the building of the ark of the Old Testament, we perceived and knew that in five thousand years and a half (one thousand) years, Jesus Christ was to come in the ark or tabernacle of a body;

14. And so our scriptures testify that he is the son of God, and the Lord and King of Israel.

15. And because after his suffering, our chief priests were surprised at the signs which were wrought by his means, we opened that book to search all the generations down to the

generation of Joseph and Mary the mother of Jesus, supposing him to be of the seed of David;

16. And we found the account of the creation, and at what time he made the heaven and the earth and the first man Adam, and that from thence to the flood, were two thousand, two hundred and twelve years.

17. And from the flood to Abraham, nine hundred and twelve. And from Abraham to Moses, four hundred and thirty. And from Moses to David the king, five hundred and ten.

18. And from David to the Babylonish captivity, five hundred years. And from the Babylonish captivity to the incarnation of Christ, four hundred years.

19. The sum of all which amounts to five thousand and half (a thousand).

20. And so it appears, that Jesus whom we crucified, is Jesus Christ the Son of God, and true and Almighty God. Amen.

What a Sacrifice
A poem by Sis. Halima

Oh what a sacrifice you gave to me
You gave your life so that I can be free
Oh what a sacrifice to come down on earth
You died on the cross
Especially for my rebirth
Oh what a sacrifice to be beat just for me
Took away all my sins and gave me eternity
There's no one who compares
With the life that you gave
Whosoever will come you allows to be saved
There's no money to give
For the price that you paid
Give you honor and praise
For that new life you gave
If there's someone who doubts
And you do not believe
Take a look at your bible
You will see as you read
He's the one who's called Christ
The only one who can save
He took our sins on his shoulders
And His life he gave
He's the one who left all
To die for you and for me
He tells the devils "depart"
They have no choice but to flee
He lets us know He's the door
And there's no price to come in
He lets us see victory
And in the end, we will win

I am the door: if any man enter in, He shall be saved,
And shall go in and out, and find pasture.
—John 10:9

There is no fact in history more clearly established than the fact of the "First Coming" of Christ. But as His "First Coming" did not fulfill all the prophecies associated with His "Coming," it is evident that there must be another "Coming" to completely fulfill them.

It was because the religious leaders of Christ's day failed to distinguish between the prophecies that related to His "First Coming," and those that related to His "Second Coming" that they rejected Him.

Peter tells us (1 Pet. 1:10–11) that the prophets themselves did not clearly perceive the difference between the "Sufferings" and "Glory" of Christ. That is, they did not see that there was a "Time Space" between the "Cross" and the "Crown", and that the "Cross" would precede the "Crown."

But we have no such excuse. We live on this side of the "Cross," and we can readily pick out all the prophecies that were fulfilled at Christ's "First Coming" and apply the remainder to His "Second Coming."

It is clear then that Christ's "First Coming," important as it was, is not the "doctrinal center" of the Scriptures—that is, Christ's "First Coming" was not the center of a circle that contains all doctrine, but was one of the foci of an ellipse of which the other is the "Second Coming."

"In My Father's House are many mansions: if it were not so, I would have told you. I go to prepare a place for you. And if I go and prepare a place for you, *I will come again*, and receive you unto myself; that where I am, there ye may be also" (John 14:2–3; emphasis mine).

For as Jonas was three days and three nights in the whale's belly; so shall the Son of man be three days and three nights in the heart of the earth (Matt. 12:40).

There is one body, and one Spirit, even as ye are called in one hope of your calling; One Lord, one faith, one baptism, One God and Father of all, who is above all, and through all, and in you all. But unto every one of us is given grace according to the measure of the gift of Christ. Wherefore he saith, When he ascended up on high, he led captivity captive, and gave gifts unto men.

Now that he ascended, what is it but that he also descended first into the lower parts of the earth? He that descended is the same also that ascended up far above all heavens, that he might fill all things. *[Eph. 4:4–10]*

2

Prepare to Receive Jesus

All Things through Christ
A poem by Sis. Halima

When the world just keeps on pounding
On your burdens that's already here.
When the doors you come to
Are closing before you
And your heart is filled only with fear.
When you see this world around you
Collapsing before your very eyes.
And the only thing that your ears hear
Is the suffering of human cries.

There's someone who wants me to tell you.
Through our weakness he will be our strength.
They'll be times when we cry, we must realize
Jesus Christ our Savior has been sent.
He's been sent to take away our burdens.
He's been sent to take away our fears.
He's been sent to give us the strength to endure.
It is he that will wipe away all tears.

So if at this time you are hungry.
Or if at this time you are full.
Just know in your heart it is Christ above
That will give us the strength to endure.
It is He that will show us his mercies.
When we're up or when we are down.
It is He that has stored up the gifts of God.
They await us our own precious crowns.

I can do all things through Christ
which strengtheneth me.
—Philippians 4:13

Book of Nicodemus

Chapter XV

1. While all the saints were rejoicing, behold Satan, the prince and captain of death, said to the prince of hell,
2. Prepare to receive Jesus of Nazareth himself, who boasted that he was the Son of God, and yet was a man afraid of death, and said, My soul is sorrowful even to death.
3. Besides he did many injuries to me and to many others; for those whom I made blind and lame and those also whom I tormented with several devils, he cured by his word; yea, and those whom I brought dead to thee, he by force takes away from thee.
4. To this the prince of hell replied to Satan, Who is that so powerful prince, and yet a man who is afraid of death?
5. For all the potentates of the earth are subject to my power, whom thou broughtest to subjection by thy power.
6. But if he be so powerful in his human nature, I affirm to thee for truth, that he is almighty in his divine nature, and no man can resist his power.
7. When therefore he said he was afraid of death, he designed to ensnare thee, and unhappy it will be to thee for everlasting ages.
8. Then Satan replying, said to the prince of hell, Why didst thou express a doubt, and wast afraid to receive that Jesus of Nazareth, both thy adversary and mine?
9. As for me, I tempted him and stirred up my old people the Jews with zeal and anger against him.
10. I sharpened the spear for his suffering; I mixed the gall and vinegar, and commanded that he should drink it; I prepared the cross to crucify him, and the nails to pierce through his hands and feet; and now his death is near at hand, I will bring him hither, subject both to thee and me.
11. Then the prince of hell answering, said, Thou saidest to me just now, that he took away the dead from me by force.

12. They who have been kept here till they should live again upon earth, were taken away hence, not by their own power, but by prayers made to God, and their almighty God took them from me.
13. Who then is that Jesus of Nazareth that by his word hath taken away the dead from me without prayer to God?
14. Perhaps it is the same who took away from me Lazarus, after he had been four days dead, and did both stink and was rotten, and of whom I had possession as a dead person, yet he brought him to life again by his power.
15. Satan answering, replied to the prince of hell, It is the very same person, Jesus of Nazareth.
16. Which when the prince of hell heard, he said to him, I adjure thee by the powers which belong to thee and me, that thou bring him not to me.
17. For when I heard of the power of his word, I trembled for fear, and all my impious company were at the same time disturbed;
18. And we were not able to detain Lazarus, but he gave himself a shake, and with all the signs of malice, he immediately went away from us; and the very earth, in which the dead body of Lazarus was lodged, presently turned him out alive.
19. And I know now that he is Almighty God who could perform such things, who is mighty in his dominion, and mighty in his human nature, who is the Saviour of mankind.
20. Bring not therefore this person hither, for he will set at liberty all those whom I hold in prison under unbelief, and bound with the fetters of their sins, and will conduct them to everlasting life.

Chapter XVI

1. And while Satan and the prince of hell were discoursing thus to each other, on a sudden there was a voice as of thunder and the rushing winds, saying lift up your gates,

O ye princes: and be ye lift up, O everlasting gates, and the King of Glory shall come in.

2. When the prince of hell heard this, he said to Satan, Depart from me, and begone out of my habitations; if thou art a powerful warrior, fight with the King of Glory. But what hast thou to do with him?

3. And he cast him forth from his habitations.

4. And the prince said to his impious officers, Shut the brass gates of cruelty, and make them fast with iron bars, and fight courageously, lest we be taken captives.

5. But when all the company of the saints heard this they spake with a loud voice of anger to the prince of hell:

6. Open thy gates that the King of Glory may come in.

7. And the divine prophet David, cried out saying, Did not I when on earth truly prophesy and say, O that men would praise the Lord for his goodness, and for his wonderful works to the children of men.

8. For he hath broken the gates of brass, and cut the bars of iron in sunder. He hath taken them because of their iniquity, and because of their unrighteousness they are afflicted.

9. After this another prophet, namely, Holy Isaiah, spake in like manner to all the saints, did not I rightly prophesy to you when I was alive on earth?

10. The dead men shall live, and they shall rise again who are in their graves, and they shall rejoice who are in earth; for the dew which is from the Lord shall bring deliverance to them.

11. And I said in another place, O death, where is thy victory? O death, where is thy sting?

12. When all the saints heard these things spoken by Isaiah, they said to the prince of hell, Open now thy gates, and take away thine iron bars; for thou wilt now be bound, and have no power.

13. Then there was a great voice, as of the sound of thunder saying, Lift up your gates, 0, princes; and be ye lifted up, ye gates of hell, and the King of Glory will enter in.

14. The prince of hell perceiving the same voice repeated, cried out as though he had been ignorant, Who is that King of Glory?

15. David replied to the prince of hell, and said, I understand the words of that voice, because I spake them by his spirit. And now, as I have above said, I say unto thee, the Lord strong and powerful, the Lord mighty in battle: he is the King of Glory, and he is the Lord in heaven and in earth;

16. He hath looked down to hear the groans of the prisoners, and to set loose those that are appointed to death.

17. And now, thou filthy and stinking prince of hell, open thy gates, that the King of Glory may enter in; for he is the Lord of heaven and earth.

18. While David was saying this, the mighty Lord appeared in the form of a man, and enlightened those places which had ever before been in darkness,

19. And broke asunder the fetters which before could not be broken; and with his invincible power visited those who sat in the deep darkness by iniquity, and the shadow of death by sin.

Chapter XVII

1. *Impious* Death and her cruel officers hearing these things, were seized with fear in their several kingdoms, when they saw the clearness of the light,

2. And Christ Himself on a sudden appearing in their habitations; they cried out therefore, and said, We are bound by thee; thou seemest to intend our confusion before the Lord.

3. Who art thou, who hast no sign of corruption, but that bright appearance which is a full proof of thy greatness, of which yet thou seemest to take no notice?

4. Who art thou, so powerful and so weak, so great and so little, a mean and yet a soldier of the first rank, who can command in the form of a servant as a common soldier?

5. The King of Glory, dead and alive, though once slain upon the cross?

6. Who layest dead in the grave, and art come down alive to us, and in thy death all the creatures trembled, and all the stars were moved, and now hast thou thy liberty among the dead, and givest disturbance to our legions?

7. Who art thou, who dost release the captives that were held in chains by original sin, and bringest them into their former liberty?

8. Who art thou, who dost spread so glorious and divine a light over those who were made blind by the darkness of sin?

9. In like manner all the legions of devils were seized with the like horror, and with the most submissive fear cried out, and said,

10. Whence comes it, 0, thou Jesus Christ, that thou art a man so powerful and glorious in majesty, so bright as to have no spot, and so pure as to have no crime? For that lower world of earth, which was ever till now subject to us, and from whence we received tribute, never sent us such a dead man before, never sent such presents as these to the princes of hell.

11. Who therefore art thou, who with such courage enterest among our abodes, and art not only not afraid to threaten us with the greatest punishments, but also endeavourest to rescue all others from the chains in which we hold them?

12. Perhaps thou art that Jesus, of whom Satan just now spoke to our prince, that by the death of the cross thou wert about to receive the power of death.

13. Then the King of Glory trampling upon death, seized the prince of hell, deprived him of all his power, and took our earthly father Adam with him to his glory.

Chapter XVIII

1. Then the prince of hell took Satan, and with great indignation said to him, O thou prince of destruction, author of Beelzebub's defeat and banishment, the scorn of God's angels and loathed by all righteous persons! What inclined thee to act thus?

2. Thou wouldst crucify the King of Glory, and by his destruction, hast made us promises of very large advantages, but as a fool wert ignorant of what thou wast about.

3. For behold now that Jesus of Nazareth, with the brightness of his glorious divinity, puts to flight all the horrid powers of darkness and death;

4. He has broken down our prisons from top to bottom, dismissed all the captives, released all who were bound, and all who were wont formerly to groan under the weight of their torments have now insulted us, and we are like to be defeated by their prayers.

5. Our impious dominions are subdued, and no part of mankind is now left in our subjection, but on the other hand, they all boldly defy us;

6. Though, before, the dead never durst behave themselves insolently towards us, nor, being prisoners, could ever on any occasion be merry.

7. O Satan, thou prince of all the wicked, father of the impious and abandoned, why wouldest thou attempt this exploit, seeing our prisoners were hitherto always without the least hopes of salvation and life?

8. But now there is not one of them does ever groan, nor is there the least appearance of a tear in any of their faces.

9. O prince Satan, thou great keeper of the infernal regions, all thy advantages which thou didst acquire by the forbidden tree, and the loss of Paradise, thou hast now lost by the wood of the cross;

10. And thy happiness all then expired, when thou didst crucify Jesus Christ the King of Glory.

11. Thou hast acted against thine own interest and mine as thou wilt presently perceive by those large torments and infinite punishments which thou art about to suffer.

12. O Satan, prince of all evil, author of death, and source of all pride, thou shouldest first have inquired into the evil crimes of Jesus of Nazareth, and then thou wouldest have found that he was guilty of no fault worthy of death.

13. Why didst thou venture, without either reason or justice, to crucify him, and hast brought down to our regions a person innocent and righteous, and thereby hast lost all the sinners, impious and unrighteous persons in the whole world?

14. While the prince of hell was thus speaking to Satan, the King of Glory said to Beelzebub, the prince of hell, Satan, the prince shall be subject to thy dominion forever, in the room of Adam and his righteous sons, who are mine.

Chapter XIX

2. Then Jesus stretched forth his hand, and said, Come to me, all ye my saints, who were created in my image, who were condemned by the tree of forbidden fruit, and by the devil and death;

3. Live now by the wood of my cross; the devil, the prince of this world, is overcome, and death is conquered.

4. Then presently all the saints were joined together under the hand of the most high God; and the Lord Jesus laid hold on Adam's hand and said to him, Peace be to thee, and all thy righteous posterity, which is mine.

5. Then Adam, casting himself at the feet of Jesus, addressed himself to Him, with tears, in humble language, and a loud voice, saying,

6. I will extol thee, O Lord, for thou hast lifted me up, and hast not made my foes to rejoice over me. O Lord my God, I cried unto thee, and thou hast healed me.

7. O Lord thou hast brought up my soul from the grave; thou hast kept me alive, that I should not go down to the pit.

8. Sing unto the Lord, all ye saints of His, and give thanks at the remembrance of His Holiness. For his anger endureth but for a moment; in his favour is life.

9. In like manner all the saints, prostrate at the feet of Jesus, said with one voice, Thou art come, O Redeemer of the world, and hast actually accomplished all things, which thou didst foretell by the law and thy holy prophets.

10. Thou hast redeemed the living by thy cross, and art come down to us, that by the death of the cross thou mightest deliver us from hell, and by thy power from death.10. O, Lord, as thou hast put the ensigns of thy glory in heaven, and hast set up the sign of praise, and followed the Lord.

11. Then the Lord stretching forth His hand, made the sign of the cross upon Adam, and upon all His saints.

12. And taking hold of Adam by his right hand, He ascended from hell, and all the saints of God followed Him.

13. Then the royal prophet David boldly cried, and said, O sing unto the Lord a new song, for he hath done marvelous things; His right hand and His holy arm have gotten Him the victory.

14. The Lord hath made His salvation, His righteousness hath He openly shewn in the sight of the heathen.

15. And the whole multitude of saints answered, saying, This honour have all His saints, Amen, Praise ye the Lord.

16. Afterwards, the prophet Habakkuk cried out, and said, Thou wentest forth for the salvation of thy people, even for this, behold there came another the salvation of thy people.

17. And all the saints said, Blessed is he who cometh in the name of the Lord; for the Lord hath enlightened us. This is our God for ever and ever; He shall reign over us to everlasting ages, Amen.

18. In like manner all the prophets spake the sacred things of His praise, and followed the Lord.

Chapter XX

1. Then the Lord holding Adam by the hand, delivered him to Michael the archangel; and he led them into Paradise, filled with mercy and glory;

2. And two very ancient men met them, and were asked by the saints, Who are you, who have not yet been with us in hell, and have had your bodies placed in Paradise?

3. One of them answering, said, I am Enoch, who was translated by the word of God: and this man who is with me, is Elijah the Tishbite, who was translated in a fiery chariot.

4. Here we have hitherto been and have not tasted death, but are now about to return at the coming of Antichrist, being armed with divine signs and miracles, to engage with him in battle, and to be slain by him at Jerusalem, and to be taken up alive again into the clouds, after three days and a half.

5. And while the holy Enoch and Elijah were relating this, behold there came another man in a miserable figure carrying the sign of the cross upon his shoulders.

6. And when all the saints saw him, they said to him, Who art thou? For thy countenance is like a thief's; and why dost thou carry a cross upon thy shoulders?

7. To which he answering, said, Ye say right, for I was a thief, who committed all sorts of wickedness upon earth.

8. And the Jews crucified me with Jesus; and I observed the surprising things which happened in the creation at the crucifixion of the Lord Jesus.

9. And I believed him to be the Creator of all things, and the Almighty King; and I prayed to him, saying, Lord, remember me, when thou comest into thy kingdom.

10. He presently regarded my supplication, and said to me, Verily I say unto thee, this day thou shalt be with me in Paradise.

11. And he gave me this sign of the cross saying, Carry this, and go to Paradise; and if the angel who is the guard of Paradise will not admit thee, shew him the sign of the cross, and say unto him: Jesus Christ who is now crucified, hath sent me hither to thee.

12. When I did this, and told the angel who is the guard of Paradise all these things, and he heard them, he presently opened the gates, introduced me, and placed me on the right-hand in paradise,

13. Saying, Stay here a little time, till Adam, the father of all mankind, shall enter in, with all his sons, who are the holy and righteous servants of Jesus Christ, who was crucified.

14. When they heard all this account from the thief, all the patriarchs said with one voice, Blessed be thou, O, Almighty God, the Father of everlasting goodness, and the Father of mercies, who hast shewn such favour to those who were sinners against him, and hast brought them to the mercy of Paradise, and hast placed them amidst thy large and spiritual provisions, in a spiritual and holy life. Amen.

The Virtue of Patience
A poem by Sis. Halima

Patience is a virtue
That's what people always say
If you have the patience of the Lord
He'll keep you from day to day
Virtue is a gift
Only the Lord above can give
He gives virtue from His Only Son
The kind that makes us live
Patience makes us humble
Keeps us looking up above
Asking strength and guidance from the Lord
To lead us with His love
Virtue is a blessing
Gives you strength from deep within
Lets you have the patience to endure
The disappointment of sin
If you have the patience of the Lord
And you know that you should
You'll believe the things the Lord has said
That all things work together for good

And we know that all things work together
for good to them that love God,
to them who are the called according to his purpose.
—Romans 8:28

For this we say unto you by the word of the Lord, that we which are alive and remain unto the coming of the Lord shall not prevent them which are asleep. For the Lord Himself shall descend from heaven with a shout, with the voice of the arch angel, and with the trump of God: and the dead in Christ shall rise first: Then we which are alive and remain shall be caught up together with them in the clouds, to meet the Lord in the air: and so shall we ever be with the Lord. Wherefore comfort one another with these words. *(1 Thess. 4:15–18)*

3

The Rapture

I Want to See Jesus
A poem by Sis. Halima

While on my dying bed I know
The time has come for me to go
I see my family all about
But they knew it was time for me to check out
I wonder if my Lord would meet me
Or would He have someone else to greet me
I wonder if He'd take my hand
And show me all His beautiful land
And then I thought it could be so
Another saint would come that I know
It could be Moses with his rod
And with him Aaron by his side
It could be Joshua with his spear
Or Ruth and Naomi meeting me there
It could be David with his son
You know the one, Solomon
And then I thought for a while
I'd like to see Jesus with His smile
I'd like to see Jesus come to me
I'd like to hear Him tell me I'm free
I'd like to know that He'll be there
And let me know that someone cares

We are confident I say and willing
rather to be absent from the body
and to be present with the Lord.
                              —2 Corinthians 5:6

The Rapture

The Rapture is described in 1 Thessalonians 4:

> For this we say unto you by the word of the Lord, that we which are alive and remain unto the coming of the Lord shall not prevent them which are asleep. For the Lord *Himself* shall descend from heaven with a shout, with the voice of the Archangel (Michael) and with the *trump of God*; and the *Dead in Christ shall rise first*; then we which are *alive and remain* (saints only) shall be caught up together with them in the clouds, to meet the Lord *in the air*, and so shall we ever be with the Lord. (1 Thess. 4:15–17; emphasis mine)

From this, we see that "the Rapture" will be *twofold*.

1. The Resurrection of the "Dead in Christ."
2. The Translation of the "Living Saints."

This twofold character of "the Rapture" Jesus revealed to Martha when He was about to raise her brother Lazarus. He said to her:

> *I am the 'Resurrection and the Life*, he that believeth in *Me, though he were dead* yet shall He live (First Resurrection Saints); and whosoever liveth (is alive when I come back) and believeth in *Me shall* "Never Die." (John 11:25–26; emphasis mine)

This twofold character of The Rapture, Paul emphasizes in his immortal chapter on the Resurrection.

> Behold, I show you a *Mystery*, we shall not all *Sleep*, but we shall *All Be Changed* in a moment, in the twinkling of an eye, at the last trump; for

the trumpet shall sound, and the *dead* shall be *raised* and *we* shall be *changed*. For this *Corruptible* (the dead in Christ) must put on *incorruption*, and this *mortal* (the living saints) must put on *immortality*. So when this *corruptible* shall have put on *incorruption*, and this *mortal* shall have put on *immortality*, then shall be brought to pass the saying that is written, *death is swallowed up in victory. O death, where is thy sting? O grave, where is thy victory?* (1 Cor. 15:51–57)

In 2 Corinthians 5:1–4, Paul expresses his longing, and the longing of the Saints, to be among those who should not be "unclothed" by Death, but who should be "clothed upon" by Immortality "without dying."

"For we know that if our earthly house of this tabernacle (the body), were *dissolved* (that is die), we have a building of God, a house not made with hands eternal in the heavens. For in this (body) we groan, earnestly desiring to be 'clothed upon' with our house which is from heaven; if so be that being 'clothed' we shall not be found naked. For we that are in this tabernacle (the body) do groan, being burdened; not for that we would be 'unclothed' (by death), but 'clothed upon' (by immortality), that 'mortality' might be swallowed up of life."

In his letter to the Philippians, while Paul hopes that "If by any means he may attain unto the (out from among the dead) *Resurrection*, yet he pressed toward the mark for the 'prize' of the High (out and up) Calling of God in Christ Jesus" (Phil. 3:11–14).

That is, while Paul would esteem it a great thing to "rise from the dead" at the First Resurrection, and be "caught up" with those who should be "changed," yet he would esteem it a "prize" if he could be caught up "without dying," that is, live until Jesus came back.

The Rapture Will Be a "Surprise"

> Watch therefore; for ye know not what hour your Lord doth come. But know this, that if the Goodman of the house had known in what watch the thief would come, he would have watched, and would not have suffered his house to be broken up. Therefore be ye also ready; for in such an hour as ye think not, the Son of Man cometh. (Matt. 24:42–44)

> Behold, I come as a thief. Blessed is he that watcheth, and keepeth his garments, lest he walk naked, and they see his shame. (Rev. 16:15)

"But of the 'times' and the 'seasons' brethren, ye have no need that I write unto you. For yourselves know perfectly that the 'Day of the Lord' (the day of His Return), so cometh as a thief in the night. For when they shall say, 'Peace and Safety;' then sudden destruction cometh upon them as travail upon a woman with child, and they shall not escape."

This refers to the Second Stage of Christ's Coming, "the Revelation," when He shall take vengeance upon His enemies (2 Thess. 1:7–10). But Paul adds: "But ye, brethren, are not in darkness, that that day (the day of His return) should overtake you as a thief" (1 Thess. 5:1–4).

We see from this that when Christ comes back, it will be when we are not expecting Him. He will come as a thief comes. A thief does not announce his coming. He comes for a certain purpose. He does not take everything there is in the house. He takes only the precious things, the jewels, the gold, the silver, and fine-wearing apparel. He does not come to stay. As soon as he secures what he is after, he departs.

So Jesus at the Rapture will come and take away the saints only. The thief leaves much more than he takes. He leaves the house and the furniture and the household utensils. So the Lord at the Rapture will leave the wicked and the great mass of the heathen behind, for those who will be taken will be comparatively few. We must not forget in our study of this subject that there are to be two resurrections of the dead. The first, of the Righteous dead before the Millennium, and the second of the wicked dead after the millennium (Rev. 20:4–6).

The Rapture Will Be "Elective"

It will not only separate the saints from unbelievers, but it will separate husbands from wives, brothers from sisters, friends from friends.

> I tell you, in that night there shall be two men in one bed; the one shall be taken, and the other shall be left. Two *women* shall be grinding together; the one shall be taken, and the other left. Two *men* shall be in the field; the one shall be taken, and the other left. (Luke 1 7:34–36)

The words "men" and "women" in this passage are in italics. That means that they are not in the original, and so the passage should read there shall be "two in one bed," husband and wife, or two brothers, or two sisters, or two friends. Two in "bed" indicates night; two grinding at the mill, morning or evening; two in the field mid-noon. This shows that the Rapture will happen all over the earth at the same time or as the apostle describes it in a "moment," or the "twinkling of an eye." As the lightning cometh out of the east, and shineth even unto the west; so shall also the coming of the Son of Man Be" (Matt. 24:27) is the way Jesus puts it.

The "Rapture" will be the most startling "event" of this age and dispensation. As it is to occur in the "twinkling of an eye" and all over the earth at the same time, that part of the world that is not asleep will witness the event. As to the "Shout of the Lord," the "Voice of the Archangel," and the "Trump of God", we do not know whether their sound will be heard and distinguished by others than the "dead in Christ" and the "living saints." We know that one day the Father spoke to Christ in a voice that He understood, but the people who stood by mistook it for "thunder" (John 12:28–29). When the Lord appeared to Saul of Tarsus on the road to Damascus and spoke to him, the men that journeyed with him stood speechless, "hearing a voice," but seeing no man, and not understanding what was said (Acts 9:3–7).

At first, the whole thing will be a Mystery, until someone who had heard or read about the "Rapture of the Saints," realizing what has happened, will explain the situation.

But one of the surprises of that day will be that so many professing Christians, and among them many ministers and Christian workers, will be left behind, while some who were not known to be Christians will be missing.

The next day's papers will be full of what happened the day before, and many of them will be swelled to twice their ordinary size by the pressure on their advertising columns for information as to missing ones, and for help to fill important vacancies and positions of trust.

For a few days, the excitement will be intense. Then the people will settle down to the inevitable. With the exception of a few who will repent and turn to God, the mass of the people will become more hardened and wicked than before, and some who lost loved ones will be embittered.

It is immediately after the sealing of the 144,000 from the tribes of Israel that John described what some believe is the great multitude of newly-raptured saints in heaven.

They will be "from every nation, tribe, people and language, standing before the throne and in front of the Lamb," holding palm branches (just as the great crowd had done during Jesus's triumphal entry into Jerusalem on Passover (John 12:12–13) and praising God (Rev. 7:9–17).

This multitude of saved believers will have been caught up, dead and alive, out of the Great Tribulation (7:14). As a result, they will not have to endure the wrath of God during the Day of the Lord period, most of which will consist of the Trumpet Judgments.

The Day of the Lord will begin, as written chronologically in the Book of Revelation, after the opening of the Seventh Seal (8:1–10:7), when God no longer will be "passive" (in opening the seals) but, rather, will take an active role in directing angels to dispense His wrath upon the earth.

The Rapture will be such an extraordinarily stupendous and unique event in human history that one certainly would have expected Jesus to have foreseen, and John to have viewed, its future happening.

Some believe Jesus did so when He described the coming of the Son of Man on the clouds of the sky (Matt. 24:30–31), and John did so during his description of the Sixth Seal events (Rev. 6:16), as well as of the "great multitude that no one could count, from every nation, tribe, people and language" soon thereafter in heaven (Rev. 7:9).

What a Great Reunion
A poem by Sis. Halima

What a great reunion…it will truly be,
to stand together…with our family.
To stand and know…the time has come,
The Creator has made…our family as one.
What a great reunion…everyone will rejoice,
no more tears—no more sorrow
we'll give praises with our voice,
We'll give honor and blessings
to the Creator above…for preserving our souls
with commitment and love
What a great reunion…I know I'll be there,
Christ paid the price…and made me His heir.
I'll see Moses and Aaron
Yes I'll see Esther too
I'll see Malcolm and Martin
You'll see me—-I'll see you
What a great reunion…our Lord has prepared,
Only those with faith…in our Lord will be there.
Only those who will hear…the roll call of his voice
but the best part of it all…is that we all have a choice.

And God shall wipe away all tears from their
eyes; and there shall be no more death,
neither sorrow, nor crying, neither
shall there be any more pain:
for the former things are passed away.
—Revelation 20:4

And Enoch lived sixty and five years, and begat Methuselah: And Enoch walked with God after he begat Methuselah three hundred years, and begat sons and daughters: And all the days of Enoch were three hundred sixty and five years: And Enoch walked with God: and he was not; *for God took him. (Gen. 5:21–24; emphasis mine)*

4

The Book of the Secrets of Enoch

Enoch was born on the sixth day of the month Tsivan and lived 365 years. He was taken up to heaven on the first day of the month Tsivan and remained in heaven sixty days. He wrote all these signs of all creation, which the Lord created, and wrote 366 books and handed them over to his sons and remained on earth thirty days and was again taken up to heaven on the sixth day of the month Tsivan, on the very day and hour when he was born (Enoch LXVIII).

He is also identified as the apostle Idris in Arabic.

How I Think of Thee
A poem by Sis. Halima

When I think about my Lord
I never ever, ever get bored
I think about how He saved me
Released me from the devil and set me free.
I think about how He gave me
The tree of life and eternity.
I think of the things that I have done
The sins, the lies, the frustrations.
And then I knew without a doubt
Only the Lord Jesus could pull me out.
I called my mother, my brother too
But sin had them both stuck like glue.
My friends, my foes, they call to me
I send them to Jesus, He sets them free.
I tell them if they have a doubt,
Read about Jesus, check Him out.
The saints of old they did the same
They found out he wasn't playing no games.
When Noah heard about the flood
He knew my Lord would surround him with love.
When Daniel was thrown into the lion's den
He had already confessed all his sins.
When Peter heard the clock strike three
He said in his heart Lord forgive me.
I believe the Lord Jesus forgave him too
And if you ask him, He'll forgive you

Ask, and it shall be given you; seek, and ye shall
find; knock and it shall be opened unto you:
for every one that asketh receiveth:
and he that seeketh findeth:
and to him that knocketh it shall be opened.
—Matthew 7:7

This new fragment of early literature came to light through certain manuscripts which were recently found in Russia and Servia and so far as is yet known has been preserved only in Slavonic. Little is known of its origin except that in its present form, it was written somewhere about the beginning of the Christian era. Its final editor was a Greek and the place of its composition Egypt. Its value lies in the unquestioned influence which it has exerted on the writers of the New Testament. Some of the dark passages of the latter being all but inexplicable without its aid.

Although the very knowledge that such a book ever existed was lost for probably 1,200 years, it nevertheless was much used by both Christian and heretic in the early centuries and forms a most valuable document in any study of the forms of early Christianity.

The writing appeals to the reader who thrills to lend wings to his thoughts and fly to mystical realms. Here is a strange dramatization of eternity—with views on Creation, Anthropology, and Ethics. As the world was made in six days, so its history would be accomplished in six thousand years, and this would be followed by a thousand years of rest (possibly when the balance of conflicting moral forces has been struck and human life has reached the ideal state). At its close would begin the eighth Eternal Day, when time should be no more.

I.

An account of the mechanism of the world showing the machinery of the sun and moon in operation. Astronomy and an interesting ancient calendar. See chapter 15–17, also 21. What the world was like before Creation, see chapter 24. Chapter 26 is especially picturesque. A unique account of how Satan was created (chapter 29).

1. There was a wise man, a great artificer, and the Lord conceived love for him and received him, that he should behold the uppermost dwellings and be an eye-witness of the wise and great and inconceivable and immutable realm of God Almighty, of the very wonderful and glorious and bright and many-eyed station of the Lord's servants, and of

the inaccessible throne of the Lord, and of the degrees and manifestations of the incorporeal hosts, and of the ineffable ministration of the multitude of the elements, and of the various apparition and inexpressible singing of the host of Cherubim, and of the boundless light.

2. At that time, he said, when my 165th year was completed, I begat my son Mathusal.

3. After this too, I lived two hundred years and completed of all the years of my life three hundred and sixty-five years.

4. On the first day of the first month I was in my house alone and was resting on my couch and slept.

5. And when I was asleep, great distress came up into my heart, and I was weeping with my eyes in sleep, and I could not understand what this distress was, or what would happen to me.

6. And there appeared to me two men, exceeding big, so that I never saw such on earth; their faces were shining like the sun, their eyes too were like a burning light, and from their lips was fire coming forth with clothing and singing of various kinds in appearance purple, their wings were brighter than gold, their hands whiter than snow.

7. They were standing at the head of my couch and began to call me by my name.

8. And I arose from my sleep and saw clearly those two men standing in front of me.

9. And I saluted them and was seized with fear and the appearance of my face was changed from terror, and those men said to me:

10. Have courage, Enoch, do not fear; the eternal God sent us to thee, and lo! thou shalt today ascend with us into heaven, and thou shalt tell thy sons and all thy household all that they shall do without thee on earth in thy house, and let no one seek thee till the Lord return thee to them.

11. And I made haste to obey them and went out from my house, and made to the doors, as it was ordered me, and summoned my sons Mathusal and Regim and Gaidad

and made known to them all the marvels those men had told me.

II.
The instruction. How Enoch instructed his sons.

Listen to me, my children, I know not whether I go, or what will befall me; now therefore, my children, I tell you: turn not from God before the face of the vain, who made not Heaven and earth, for these shall perish and those who worship them, and may the Lord make confident your hearts in the fear of Him. And now, my children, let no one think to seek me, until the Lord return me to you.

III.
Of Enoch's assumption; how the angels took him into the first heaven.

It came to pass, when Enoch had told his sons, that the angels took him on to their wings and bore him up on to the first heaven and placed him on the clouds. And there I looked, and again I looked higher, and saw the ether, and they placed me on the first heaven and showed me a very great sea, greater than the earthly sea.

IV.
Of the Angels ruling the stars.

They brought before my face the elders and rulers of the stellar orders, and showed me two hundred angels, who rule the stars and their services to the heavens, and fly with their wings and come around all those who sail.

V.
Of how the Angels keep the store-houses of the snow.

And here I looked down and saw the treasure-houses of the snow, and the angels who keep their terrible store-houses, and the clouds whence they come out and into which they go.

VI.

Of the dew and of the olive-oil, and various flowers.

1. They showed me the treasure-house of the dew, like oil
    of the olive, and the appearance of its form, as of all the
    flowers of the earth; further many angels guarding the trea-
    sure-houses of these things, and how they are made to shut
    and open.

VII.

Of how Enoch was taken on to the second heaven.

1. And those men took me and led me up on to the second
    heaven, and showed me darkness, greater than earthly dark-
    ness, and there I saw prisoners hanging, watched, awaiting
    the great and boundless judgement, and these angels were
    dark-looking, more than earthly darkness, and incessantly
    making weeping through all hours.
2. And I said to the men who were with me: "Wherefore are
    these incessantly tortured?" They answered me: "These are
    God's apostates, who obeyed not God's commands, but
    took counsel with their own will, and turned away with
    their prince, who also is fastened on the fifth heaven."
3. And I felt great pity for them, and they saluted me, and
    said to me: "Man of God, pray for us to the Lord"; and I
    answered to them: "Who am I, a mortal man, that I should
    pray for angels? Who knoweth whither I go, or what will
    befall me? Or who will pray for me?"

VIII.

Of the assumption of Enoch to the third heaven.

1. And those men took me thence, and led me up on to the
    third heaven, and placed me there; and I looked down-
    wards, and saw the produce of these places, such as has
    never been known for goodness.

2. And I saw all the sweet-flowering trees and beheld their fruits, which were sweet-smelling, and all the foods borne by them bubbling with fragrant exhalation.

3. And in the midst of the trees that of life, in that place where on the Lord rests, when he goes up into paradise; and this tree is of ineffable goodness and fragrance, and adorned more than every existing thing; and on all sides it is in form gold-looking and vermilion and fire-like and covers all, and it has produce from all fruits.

4. Its root is in the garden at the earth's end.

5. And paradise is between corruptibility and incorruptibility.

6. And two springs come out which send forth honey and milk, and their springs send forth oil and wine, and they separate into four parts, and go round with quiet course, and go down into the *Paradise of Eden*, between corruptibility and incorruptibility.

7. And thence they go forth along the earth, and have a revolution to their circle even as other elements.

8. And here there is no unfruitful tree, and every place is blessed.

9. And there are three hundred angels very bright, who keep the garden, and with incessant sweet singing and never-silent voices serve the Lord throughout all days and hours.

10. And I said: 'How very sweet is this place,' and those men said to me:

IX.

The showing to Enoch of the place of the righteous and compassionate.

1. This place, O Enoch, is prepared for the righteous, who endure all manner of offence from those that exasperate their souls, who avert their eyes from iniquity, and make righteous judgement, and give bread to the hungering, and cover the naked with clothing, and raise up the fallen, and help injured orphans, and who walk without fault before the face of the Lord, and serve Him alone, and for them is prepared this place for eternal inheritance.

X.

Here they showed Enoch the tenable place and various tortures.

1. And those two men led me upon to the Northern side, and showed me there a very terrible place, and there were all manner of tortures in that place: cruel darkness and unillumined gloom, and there is no light there, but murky fire constantly flameth aloft, and there is a fiery river coming forth, and that whole place is everywhere fire, and everywhere there is frost and ice, thirst and shivering, while the bonds are very cruel, and the angels fearful and merciless, bearing angry weapons, merciless torture, and I said:

2. "Woe, woe, how very terrible is this place."

3. And those men said to me: This place, O Enoch, is prepared for those who dishonour God, who on earth practice sin against nature, which is child-corruption after the sodomitic fashion, magic-making, enchantments and devilish witchcrafts, and who boast of their wicked deeds, stealing, lies, calumnies, envy, rancor, fornication, murder, and who, accursed, steal the souls of men, who, seeing the poor take away their goods and themselves wax rich, injuring them for other men's goods; who being able to satisfy the empty, made the hungering to die; being able to clothe, stripped the naked; and who knew not their creator, and bowed down to soulless (sc. lifeless) Gods, who cannot see nor hear, vain gods, who also built hewn images and bow down to unclean handiwork, for all these is prepared this place amongst these, for eternal inheritance.

XI.

Here they took Enoch up on to the fourth heaven
where is the course of sun and moon.

1. Those men took me, and led me up on to the fourth heaven, and showed me all the successive goings, and all the rays of the light of sun and moon.

2. And I measured their goings and compared their light, and saw that the sun's light is greater than the moon's.

3. Its circle and the wheels on which it goes always, like a wind going past with very marvelous speed, and day and night it has no rest.

4. Its passage and return are accompanied by four great stars, and each star has under it a thousand stars, to the right of the sun's wheel, and by four to the left, each having under it a thousand stars, altogether eight thousand, issuing with the sun continually.

5. And by day fifteen myriads of angels attend it, and by night a thousand.

6. And six-winged ones issue with the angels before the sun's wheel into the fiery flames, and a hundred angels kindle the sun and set it alight.

XII.
Of the very marvelous elements of the sun.

1. And I looked and saw other flying elements of the sun, whose names are Phoenixes and Chalkydri, marvelous and wonderful, with feet and tails in the form of a lion, and a crocodile's head, their appearance is empurpled, like the rainbow; their size is nine hundred measures, their wings are like those of angels, each has twelve, and they attend and accompany the sun, bearing heat and dew, as it is ordered them from God.

2. Thus the sun revolves and goes, and rises under the heaven, and its course goes under the earth with the light of its rays incessantly.

XIII.
The angels took Enoch and placed him in the east at the sun's gates.

1. Those men bore me away to the east, and placed me at the sun's gates, where the sun goes forth according to the

regulation of the seasons and the circuit of the months of the whole year, and the number of the hours day and night.

2. And I saw six gates open, each gate having sixty-one stadia and a quarter of one stadium, and I measured them truly, and understood their size to be so much, through which the sun goes forth, and goes to the west, and is made even, and rises throughout all the months, and turns back again from the six gates according to the succession of the seasons; thus the period of the whole year is finished after the returns of the four seasons.

XIV.
They took Enoch to the West.

1. And again those men led me away to the western parts, and showed me six great gates open corresponding to the Eastern gates, opposite to where the sun sets, according to the number of the days three hundred and sixty-five and a quarter.

2. Thus again it goes down to the western gates, and draws away its light, the greatness of its brightness, under the earth; for since the crown of its shining is in heaven with the Lord, and guarded [by four hundred angels, while the sun goes round on wheel under the earth, and stands seven great hours in night, and spends half its course under the earth, when it comes to the eastern approach in the eighth hour of the night, it brings its lights, and the crown of shining, and the sun flames forth more than fire.

XV.
The elements of the sun, the Phoenixes and Chalkydri broke into song.

1. Then the elements of the sun, called Phoenixes and Chalkydri break into song, therefore every bird flutters with its wings, rejoicing at the giver of light, and they broke into song at the command of the Lord.

2. The giver of light comes to give brightness to the whole world, and the morning guard takes shape, which is the rays of the sun, and the sun of the earth goes out, and receives its brightness to light up the whole face of the earth, and they showed me this calculation of the sun's going.

3. And the gates which it enters, these are the great gates of the computation of the hours of the year; for this reason the sun is a great creation, whose circuit lasts twenty-eight years, and begins again from the beginning.

XVI.

They took Enoch and again placed him in the east at the course of the moon.

1. Those men showed me the other course, that of the moon, twelve great gates, crowned from west to east, by which the moon goes in and out of the customary times.

2. It goes in at the first gate to the western places of the sun, by the first gates with thirty-one days exactly, by the second gates with *thirty-one days* exactly, by the third with thirty days exactly, by the fourth with thirty days exactly, by the fifth with thirty-one days exactly, by the sixth with thirty-one days exactly, by the seventh with thirty days exactly, by the eighth with thirty-one days perfectly, by the ninth with thirty-one days exactly, by the tenth with thirty days perfectly, by the eleventh with thirty-one days exactly, by the twelfth with twenty-eight days exactly.

3. And it goes through the western gates in the order and number of the eastern, and accomplishes the three hundred and sixty-five and a quarter days of the solar year, while the lunar year has three hundred and fifty-four, and there are wanting to it twelve days of the solar circle, which are the lunar epacts of the whole year.

4. Thus, too, the great circle contains five hundred and thirty-two years.

5. The quarter *of a day* is omitted for three years, the fourth fulfils *it* exactly.

6. Therefore, they are taken outside of heaven for three years and are not added to the number of days, because they change the time of the years to two new months toward completion, to two others towards diminution.

7. And when the western gates are finished, it returns and goes to the eastern to the lights, and goes thus day and night about the heavenly circles, lower than all circles, swifter than the heavenly winds, and spirits and elements and angels flying; each angel has six wings.

8. It has a sevenfold course in nineteen years.

XVII.
Of the singings of the angels, which it is impossible to describe.

In the midst of the heavens, I saw armed soldiers, serving the Lord, with tympana and organs, with incessant voice, with sweet voice, with sweet and incessant voice and various singing, which it is impossible to describe, and which astonishes every mind, so wonderful and marvelous is the singing of those angels, and I was delighted listening to it.

XVIII.
Of the taking of Enoch on to the fifth heaven.

1. The men took me on to the fifth heaven and placed me, and there I saw many and countless soldiers, called Grigori, of human appearance, and their size was greater than that of great giants and their faces withered, and the silence of their mouths perpetual, and there was no service on the fifth heaven, and I said to the men who were with me:

2. Wherefore are these very withered and their faces melancholy, and their mouths silent, and wherefore is there no service on this heaven?

3. And they said to me: These are the Grigori, who with their prince Satan, all rejected the Lord of light, and after them

are those who are held in great darkness on the second heaven, and three of them went down on to earth from the Lord's throne, to the place Ermon, and broke through their vows on the shoulder of the hill Ermon and saw the daughters of men how good they are, and took to themselves wives, and befouled the earth with their deeds, who in all times of their age made lawlessness and mixing, and giants are born and marvelous big men and great enmity.

4. And therefore God judged them with great judgement, and they weep for their brethren and they will be punished on the Lord's great day.

5. And I said to the Grigori: "I saw your brethren and their works, and their great torments, and I prayed for them, but the Lord has condemned them to be under earth till heaven and earth shall end forever."

6. And I said: "Wherefore do you wait, brethren, and do not serve before the Lord's face, and have not put your services before the Lord's face, lest you anger your Lord utterly?"

7. And they listened to my admonition, and spoke to the four ranks in heaven, and lo! As I stood with those two men four trumpets trumpeted together with great voice, and the Grigori broke into song with one voice, and their voice went up before the Lord pitifully and affectingly.

XIX.
Of the taking of Enoch on to the sixth heaven.

1. And thence those men took me and bore me up on to the sixth heaven, and there I saw seven bands of angels, very bright and very glorious, and their faces shining more than the sun's shining, glistening, and there is no difference in their faces, or behavior, or manner of dress; and these make the orders, and learn the goings of the stars, and the alteration of the moon, or revolution of the sun, and the good government of the world.

2. And when they see evildoing they make commandments and instruction, and sweet and loud singing, and all songs of praise.

3. These are the archangels who are above angels, measure all life in heaven and on earth, and the angels who are appointed over seasons and years, the angels who are over rivers and sea, and who are over the fruits of the earth, and the angels who are over every grass, giving food to all, to every living thing, and the angels who write all the souls of men, and all their deeds, and their lives before the Lord's face; in their midst are six Phoenixes and six Cherubim and six six-winged ones continually with one voice singing one voice, and it is not possible to describe their singing, and they rejoice before the Lord at his footstool.

XX.

Hence they took Enoch into the Seventh Heaven.

1. And those two men lifted me up thence on to the seventh Heaven, and I saw there a very great light, and fiery troops of great archangels, incorporeal forces, and dominions, orders and governments, cherubim and seraphim, thrones and many-eyed ones, nine regiments, the Ioanit stations of light, and I became afraid, and began to tremble with great terror, and those men took me, and led me after them, and said to me:

2. "Have courage, Enoch, do not fear," and showed me the Lord from afar, sitting on His very high throne. For what is there on the tenth heaven, since the Lord dwells here?

3. On the tenth heaven is God, in the Hebrew tongue He is called Aravat.

4. And all the heavenly troops would come and stand on the ten steps according to their rank, and would bow down to the Lord, and would again go to their places in joy and felicity, singing songs in the boundless light with small and tender voices, gloriously serving Him.

XXI.

*Of how the angels here left Enoch, at the end of the seventh Heaven,
and went away from him unseen.*

1. And the cherubim and seraphim standing about the
   throne, the six-winged and many-eyed ones do not depart,
   standing before the Lord's face doing his will, and cover his
   whole throne, singing with gentle voice before the Lord's
   face: "Holy, holy, holy, Lord Ruler of Sabaoth, heavens and
   earth are full of Thy glory."
2. When I saw all these things, those men said to me: "Enoch,
   thus far is it commanded us to journey with thee," and
   those men went away from me and thereupon I saw them
   not.
3. And I remained alone at the end of the seventh heaven
   and became afraid, and fell on my face and said to myself:
   "Woe is me, what has befallen me?"
4. And the Lord sent one of his glorious ones, the archangel
   Gabriel, and he said to me: "Have courage, Enoch, do not
   fear, arise before the Lord's face into eternity, arise, come
   with me."
5. And I answered him, and said in myself: "My Lord, my
   soul is departed from me, from terror and trembling," and
   I called to the men who led me up to this place, on them I
   relied, and it is with them I go before the Lord's face.
6. And Gabriel caught me up, as a leaf caught up by the wind,
   and placed me before the Lord's face.
7. And I saw the eighth Heaven, which is called in the Hebrew
   tongue Muzaloth, changer of the seasons, of drought, and
   of wet, and of the twelve signs of the zodiac, which are
   above the seventh Heaven.
8. And I saw the ninth Heaven, which is called in Hebrew
   Kuchavim, where are the heavenly homes of the twelve
   signs of the zodiac.

XXII.

*In the tenth Heaven, the archangel Michael
led Enoch to before the Lord's face.*

1. On the tenth Heaven, Aravoth, I saw the appearance of the Lord's face, like iron made to glow in fire, and brought out, emitting sparks, and it burns.

2. Thus I saw the Lord's face, but the Lord's face is ineffable, marvelous and very awful, and very, very terrible.

3. And who am I to tell of the Lord's unspeakable being, and of his very wonderful face? And I cannot tell the quantity of his many instructions, and various voices, the Lord's throne very great and not made with hands, nor the quantity of those standing round him, troops of cherubim and seraphim, nor their incessant singing, nor his immutable beauty, and who shall tell of the ineffable greatness of his glory?

4. And I fell prone and bowed down to the Lord, and the Lord with his lips said to me:

5. "Have courage, Enoch, do not fear, arise and stand before my face into eternity."

6. And the archistratege Michael lifted me up, and led me to before the Lord's face.

7. And the Lord said to his servants tempting them: "Let Enoch stand before my face into eternity,' and the glorious ones bowed down to the Lord, and said: "Let Enoch go according to Thy word."

8. And the Lord said to Michael: "Go and take Enoch from out his earthly garments, and anoint him with my sweet ointment, and put him into the garments of My glory."

9. And Michael did thus, as the Lord told him. He anointed me, and dressed me, and the appearance of that ointment is more than the great light, and his ointment is like sweet dew, and its smell mild, shining like the sun's ray, and I looked at myself, and was like one of his glorious ones.

10. And the Lord summoned one of his archangels by name Pravuil, whose knowledge was quicker in wisdom than the other archangels, who wrote all the deeds of the Lord; and the Lord said to Pravuil:

11. "Bring out the books from my store-houses, and a reed of quick-writing, and give it to Enoch, and deliver to him the choice and comforting books out of thy hand."

XXIII.
Of Enoch's writing, how he wrote his wonderful
journeyings and the heavenly apparitions
and himself wrote three hundred and sixty-six books.

1. And he was telling me all the works of heaven, earth and sea, and all the elements, their passages and goings, and the thunderings of the thunders, the sun and moon, the goings and changes of the stars, the seasons, years, days, and hours, the risings of the wind, the numbers of the angels, and the formation of their songs, and all human things, the tongue of every human song and life, the commandments, instructions, and sweet-voiced singings, and all things that it is fitting to learn.

2. And Pravuil told me: 'All the things that I have told thee, we have written. Sit and write all the souls of mankind, however many of them are born, and the places prepared for them to eternity; for all souls are prepared to eternity, before the formation of the world.'

3. And all double thirty days and thirty nights, and I wrote out all things exactly, and wrote three hundred and sixty-six books.

XXIV.
Of the great secrets of God, which God revealed and
told to Enoch, and spoke with him face to face.

1. And the Lord summoned me, and said to me: "Enoch, sit down on my left with Gabriel."

2. And I bowed down to the Lord, and the Lord spoke to me: Enoch, beloved, all thou seeth, all things that are standing finished I tell to thee even before the very beginning, all that I created from non-being, and visible things from invisible.

3. Hear, Enoch, and take in these my words, for not to My angels have I told my secret, and I have not told them their rise, nor my endless realm, nor have they understood my creating, which I tell thee today.

4. For before all things were visible, I alone used to go about in the invisible things, like the sun from east to west, and from west to east.

5. But even the sun has peace in itself, while I found no peace, because I was creating all things, and I conceived the thought of placing foundations, and of creating visible creation.

XXV.

God relates to Enoch, how out of the very lowest darkness comes down the visible and invisible.

1. I commanded in the very lowest parts, that visible things should come down from invisible, and Adoil came down very great, and I beheld him, and Io! he had a belly of great light.

2. And I said to him: "Become undone, Adoil, and let the visible come out of thee."

3. And he came undone, and a great light came out. And I was in the midst of the great light, and as there is born light from light, there came forth a great age, and showed all creation, which I had thought to create.

4. And I saw that it was good.

5. And I placed for myself a throne, and took my seat on it, and said to the light: "Go thou up higher and fix thyself high above the throne, and be a foundation to the highest things."

6. And above the light there is nothing else, and then I bent up and looked up from my throne.

XXVI.

*God summons from the very lowest a second time that
Archas, heavy and very red should come forth.*

1. And I summoned the very lowest a second time, and said:
   "Let Archas come forth hard," and he came forth hard
   from the invisible.
2. And Archas came forth, hard, heavy, and very red.
3. And I said: "Be opened, Archas, and let there be born from
   thee," and he came undone, an age came forth, very great
   and very dark, bearing the creation of all lower things, and
   I saw that it was good and said to him:
4. "Go thou down below, and make thyself firm, and be for a
   foundation for the lower things," and it happened and he
   went down and fixed himself, and became the foundation
   for the lower things, and below the darkness there is nothing else.

XXVII.

*Of how God founded the water, and surrounded it
with light, and established on it seven islands.*

1. And I commanded that there should be taken from light
   and darkness, and I said: "Be thick," and it became thus
   and I spread it out with the light, and it became water, and
   I spread it out over the darkness, below the light, and then
   I made firm the waters, that is to say the bottomless, and
   I made foundation of light around the water, and created
   seven circles from inside, and imaged it (sc. the water) like
   crystal wet and dry, that is to say like glass, and the cir-
   cumscriptionof the waters and the other elements, and I
   showed each one of them its road, and the seven stars each
   one of them in its heaven, that they go thus, and I saw that
   it was good.
2. And I separated between light and between darkness, that
   is to say in the midst of the water hither and thither, and I

said to the light, that it should be the day, and to the darkness, that it should be the night, and there was evening and there was morning the first day.

XXVIII.
*The week in which God showed Enoch all his wisdom
and power, throughout all the seven days,
how he created all the heavenly and earthly forces
and all moving things even down to man.*

1. And then I made firm the heavenly circle, and made that the lower water which is under heaven collect itself together, into one whole, and that the chaos become dry, and it became so.
2. Out of the waves I created rock hard and big, and from the rock I piled up the dry, and the dry I called earth, and the midst of the earth I called abyss, that is to say the bottomless, I collected the sea in one place and bound it together with a yoke.
3. And I said to the sea: "Behold I give thee thy eternal limits, and thou shalt not break loose from thy component parts."
4. Thus I made fast the firmament. This day, I called me the first-created.

XXIX.
*Then it became evening, and then again
morning, and it was the second day.
[Monday is the first day.] The fiery Essence.*

1. And for all the heavenly troops, I imaged the image and essence of fire, and my eye looked at the very hard, firm rock, and from the gleam of my eye the lightning received its wonderful nature, which is both fire in water and water in fire, and one does not put out the other, nor does the one dry up the other, therefore the lightning is brighter than the sun, softer than water and firmer than hard rock.

2. And from the rock I cutoff a great fire, and from the fire I created the orders of the incorporeal ten troops of angels, and their weapons are fiery and their raiment a burning flame, and I commanded that each one should stand in his order.

    a. *Here Satanail with his angels was thrown down from the height.*

3. And one from out the order of angels, having turned away with the order that was under him, conceived an impossible thought, to place his throne higher than the clouds above the earth, that he might become equal in rank to my power.

4. And I threw him out from the height with his angels, and he was flying in the air continuously above the bottomless.

XXX.

And then I created all the heavens, and the third day was, [Tuesday].

1. On the third day I commanded the earth to make grow great and fruitful trees, and hills, and seed to sow, and I planted Paradise, and enclosed it, and placed as armed guardians flaming angels, and thus I created renewal.

2. Then came evening, and came morning the fourth day.

3. [Wednesday]. On the fourth day, I commanded that there should be great lights on the heavenly circles.

4. On the first uppermost circle, I placed the stars, Kruno, and on the second Aphrodit, on the third Aris, on the fifth Zeus, on the sixth Ermis, on the seventh lesser the moon, and adorned it with the lesser stars.

5. And on the lower I placed the sun for the illumination of day, and the moon and stars for the illumination of night.

6. The sun that it should go according to each animal (sc. signs of the zodiac), twelve, and I appointed the succession of the months and their names and lives, their thunderings, and their hour-markings, how they should succeed.

7. Then evening came and morning came the fifth day.

8. [Thursday]. On the fifth day, I commanded the sea, that it should bring forth fishes, and feathered birds of many varieties, and all animals creeping over the earth, going forth over the earth on four legs, and soaring in the air, male sex and female, and every soul breathing the spirit of life.

9. And there came evening, and there came morning the sixth day.

10. [Friday]. On the sixth day, I commanded my wisdom to create man from seven consistencies: one, his flesh from the earth; two, his blood from the dew; three, his eyes from the sun; four, his bones from stone; five, his intelligence from the swiftness of the angels and from cloud; six, his veins and his hair from the grass of the earth; seven, his soul from my breath and from the wind.

11. And I gave him seven natures: to the flesh hearing, the eyes for sight, to the soul smell, the veins for touch, the blood for taste, the bones for endurance, to the intelligence sweetness (sc. enjoyment).

12. I conceived a cunning saying to say, I created man from invisible and from visible nature, of both are his death and life and image, he knows speech like some created thing, small in greatness and again great in smallness, and I placed him on earth, a second angel, honourable, great and glorious, and I appointed him as ruler to rule on earth and to have my wisdom, and there was none like him of earth of all my existing creatures.

13. And I appointed him a name, from the four component parts, from east, from west, from south, from north, and I appointed for him four special stars, and I called his name Adam, and showed him the two ways, the light and the darkness, and I told him:

14. "This is good, and that bad," that I should learn whether he has love towards me, or hatred, that it be clear which in his race love me.

15. For I have seen his nature, but he has not seen his own nature, therefore through not seeing he will sin worse, and I said, "After sin what is there but death?"

16. And I put sleep into him and he fell asleep. And I took from him a rib, and created him a wife, that death should come to him by his wife, and I took his last word and called her name mother, that is to say, Eva.

XXXI.

*God gives over paradise to Adam, and gives him
a command to see the heavens opened,
and that he should see the angels singing the song of victory.*

1. Adam has life on earth, and I created a garden in Eden in the east, that he should observe the testament and keep the command.

2. I made the heavens open to him, that he should see the angels singing the song of victory, and the gloomless light.

3. And he was continuously in paradise, and the devil understood that I wanted to create another world, because Adam was lord on earth, to rule and control it.

4. The devil is the evil spirit of the lower places, as a fugitive he made Sotona from the heavens as his name was Satanail, thus he became different from the angels, but his nature did not change his intelligence as far as his understanding of righteous and sinful things.

5. And he understood his condemnation and the sin which he had sinned before, therefore he conceived thought against Adam, in such form he entered and seduced Eva, but did not touch Adam.

6. But I cursed ignorance, but what I had blessed previously, those I did not curse, I cursed not man, nor the earth, nor other creatures, but man's evil fruit, and his works.

XXXII.

After Adam's sin God sends him away into
the earth "whence I took thee,"
but does not wish to ruin him for all years to come.

1. I said to him: "Earth thou art, and into the earth whence I took thee thou shalt go, and I will not ruin thee, but send thee whence I took thee."
2. Then I can again take thee at My second coming!
3. And I blessed all my creatures visible and invisible. And Adam was five and half hours in paradise.
4. And I blessed the seventh day, which is the Sabbath, on which he rested from all his works.

XXXIII.

God shows Enoch the age of this world, its
existence of seven thousand years,
and the eighth thousand is the end, neither
years, nor months, nor weeks, nor days.

1. *And I appointed the eighth day also, that the eighth day should be the first-created after my work, and that the first seven revolve in the form of the seventh thousand, and that at the beginning of the eighth thousand there* should be a time of not-counting, endless, with neither years nor months nor weeks nor days nor hours.
2. And now, Enoch, all that I have told thee, all that thou hast understood, all that thou hast seen of heavenly things, all that thou hast seen on earth, and all that I have written in books by my great wisdom, all these things I have devised and created from the uppermost foundation to the lower and to the end, and there is no counsellor nor inheritor to my creations.
3. I am self-eternal, not made with hands, and without change.

4. My thought is my counsellor, my wisdom and my word are made, and my eyes observe all things how they stand here and tremble with terror.

5. If I turn away my face, then all things will be destroyed.

6. And apply thy mind, Enoch, and know Him who is speaking to thee, and take thou the books which thou thyself hast written.

7. And I give thee Samuil and Raguil, who led thee up, and the books, and go down to earth, and tell thy sons all that I have told thee, and all that thou hast seen, from the lower heaven up to my throne, and all the troops.

8. For I created all forces, and there is none that resisteth me or that does not subject himself to me. For all subject themselves to my monarchy, and labour for my sole rule.

9. Give them the books of the handwriting, and they will read them and will know me for the creator of all things, and will understand how there is no other God but me.

10. And let them distribute the books of thy handwriting—children to children, generation to generation, nations to nations.

11. And I will give thee, Enoch, my intercessor, the archistratege Michael, for the handwritings of thy fathers Adam, Seth, Enos, Cainan, Mahaleleel, and Jared thy father.

XXXIV.

God convicts the idolaters and sodomitic fornicators,
and therefore brings down a deluge upon them.

1. They have rejected my commandments and my yoke, worthless seed has come up, not fearing God, and they would not bow down to me, but have begun to bow down to vain gods, and denied my unity, and have laden the whole earth with untruths, offences, abominable lecheries namely one with another, and all manner of other unclean wickednesses, which are disgusting to relate.

2. And therefore I will bring down a deluge upon the earth and will destroy all men, and the whole earth will crumble together into great darkness.

XXXV.
God leaves one righteous man of Enoch's tribe with his whole house, who did God's pleasure according to His will.

1. Behold from their seed shall arise another generation, much afterwards, but of them many will be very insatiate.
2. He who raises that generation, *shall* reveal to them the books of thy handwriting, of thy fathers, to them to whom he must point out the guardianship of the world, to the faithful men and workers of my pleasure, who do not acknowledge my name in vain.
3. And they shall tell another generation, and those others having read shall be glorified thereafter, more than the first.

XXXVI.
God commanded Enoch to live on earth thirty days, to give instruction to his sons and to his children's children.
After thirty days he was again taken on to heaven.

1. Now, Enoch, I give thee the term of thirty days to spend in thy house, and tell thy sons and all thy household, that all may hear from my face what is told them by thee, that they may read and understand, how there is no other God but me.
2. And that they may always keep my commandments, and begin to read and take in the books of thy handwriting.
3. And after thirty days I shall send my angel for thee, and he will take thee from earth and from thy sons to me.

XXXVII.
Here God summons an angel.

1. And the Lord called up one of the older angels, terrible and menacing, and placed him by me, in appearance white as snow, and his hands like ice, having the appearance of great frost, and he froze my face, because I could not endure the terror of the Lord, just as it is not possible to endure a stove's fire and the sun's heat, and the frost of the air.
2. And the Lord said to me: "Enoch, if thy face be not frozen here, no man will be able to behold thy face."

XXXVIII.
Mathusal continued to have hope and to await his father Enoch at his couch day and night.

1. And the Lord said to those men who first led me up: "Let Enoch go down on to earth with you, and await him till the determined day."
2. And they placed me by night on my couch.
3. And Mathusal expecting my coming, keeping watch by day and by night at my couch, was filled with awe when he heard my coming, and I told him, "Let all my household come together, that I tell them everything."

XXXIX.
Enoch's pitiful admonition to his sons with weeping and great Lamentation, as he spoke to them.

1. Oh my children, my beloved ones, hear the admonition of your father, as much as is according to the Lord's will.
2. I have been let come to you today, and announce to you, not from my lips, but from the Lord's lips, all that is and was and all that is now, and all that will be till judgement-day.
3. For the Lord has let me come to you, you hear therefore the words of my lips, of a man made big for you, but I am one

who has seen the Lord's face, like iron made to glow from fire it sends forth sparks and burns,

4. You look now upon my eyes, the eyes of a man big with meaning for you, but I have seen the Lord's eyes, shining like the sun's rays and filling the eyes of man with awe.

5. You see now, my children, the right hand of a man that helps you, but I have seen the Lord's right hand filling heaven as be helped me.

6. You see the compass of my work like your own, but I have seen the Lord's limitless and perfect compass, which has no end.

7. You hear the words of my lips, as I heard the words of the Lord, like great thunder incessantly with hurling of clouds.

8. And now, my children, hear the discourses of the father of the earth, how fearful and awful it is to come before the face of the ruler of the earth, how much more terrible and awful it is to come before the face of the ruler of heaven, the controller of quick and dead, and of the heavenly troops. Who can endure that endless pain?

XL.

Enoch admonishes his children truly of all things from the Lord's lips, how he saw and heard and wrote down.

1. And now, my children, I know all things, for this is from the Lord's lips, and this my eyes have seen, from beginning to end.

2. I know all things, and have written all things into books, the heavens and their end, and their plenitude, and all the armies and their marchings.

3. I have measured and described the stars, the great countless multitude of them.

4. What man has seen their revolutions, and their entrances? For not even the angels see their number, while I have written all their names.

5. And I measured the sun's circle, and measured its rays, counted the hours, I wrote down too all' things that go over the earth I have written the things that are nourished, and all seed sown and unsown, which the earth produces and all plants, and every grass and every flower, and their sweet smells, and their names, and the dwelling-places of the clouds, and their composition, and their wings, and how they bear rain and raindrops.

6. And I investigated all things, and wrote the road of the thunder and of the lightning, and they showed me the keys and their guardians, their rise, the way they go; it is let out in measure (sc. gently) by a chain, lest by a heavy chain and violence it hurl down the angry clouds and destroy all things on earth.

7. I wrote the treasure-houses of the snow, and the store-houses of the cold and the frosty airs, and I observed their season's key-holder, he fills the clouds with them, and does not exhaust the treasure houses.

8. And I wrote the resting-places of the winds and observed and saw how their key-holders bear weighing-scales and measures; first, they put them in one weighing-scale, then in the other the weights and let them out according to measure cunningly over the whole earth, lest by heavy breathing they make the earth to rock.

9. And I measured out the whole earth, its mountains, and all hills, fields, trees, stones, rivers, all existing things I wrote down, the height from earth to the seventh heaven, and downwards to the very lowest hell, and the judgement-place, and the very great, open and weeping hell.

10. And I saw how the prisoners are in pain, expecting the limitless judgement.

11. And I wrote down all those being judged by the judge, and all their judgements and all their works.

XLI.
Of how Enoch lamented Adam's sin.

1. And I saw all forefathers from all time with Adam and Eva, and I sighed and broke into tears and said of the ruin of their dishonour:
2. "Woe is me for my infirmity and for that of my forefathers," and thought in my, heart and said:
3. "Blessed is the man who has not been born or who has been born and shall not sin before the Lord's face, that he come not into this place, nor bring the yoke of this place!"

XLII.
Of how Enoch saw the key-holders and guards
of the gates of hell standing.

Saw the keyholders and guards of the gates of hell standing, like great serpents, and their faces like extinguished lamps, and their eyes of fire, their sharp teeth, and I saw all the Lord's works, how they are right, while the works of man are some good, and others bad, and in their works are known those who lie evilly.

XLIII.
Enoch shows his children how he measured
and wrote out God's judgments.

1. I, my children, measured and wrote out every work and every measure and every righteous judgement.
2. As one year is more honourable than another, so is one man more honourable than another, some for great possessions, some for wisdom of heart, some for particular intellect, some for cunning, one for silence of lip, another for cleanliness, one for strength, another for comeliness, one for youth, another for sharp wit, one for shape of body, another for sensibility, let it be heard everywhere, but there is none better than he who fears God, he shall be more glorious in time to come.

XLIV.

*Enoch instructs his sons, that they revile not
the face of man, small or great.*

1. The Lord with his hands having created man, in the likeness of his own face, the Lord made him small and great.
2. Whoever reviles the ruler's face, and abhors the Lord's face, has despised the Lord's face, and he who vents anger on any man without injury, the Lord's great anger will cut him down, he who spits on the face of man reproachfully, will be cut down at the Lord's great judgement.
3. Blessed is the man who does not direct his heart with malice against any man, and helps the injured and condemned, and raises the broken down, and shall do charity to the needy, because on the day of the great judgement every weight, every measure and every makeweight will be as in the market, that is to say they are hung on scales and stand in the market, and every one shall learn his own measure, and according to his measure shall take his reward.

XLV.

*God shows how he does not want from men sacrifices,
nor burnt-offerings, but pure and contrite hearts.*

1. Whoever hastens to make offering before the Lord's face, the Lord for his part will hasten that offering by granting of his work.
2. But whoever increases his lamp before the Lord's face and make not true judgement, the Lord will not increase his treasure in the realm of the highest.
3. When the Lord demands bread, or candles, or flesh (sc. cattle), or any other sacrifice, then that is nothing; but God demands pure hearts, and with all that only tests the heart of man.

XLVI.

*Of how an earthly ruler does not accept from man abominable and
unclean gifts, then how much more does God abominate unclean
gifts, but sends them away with wrath and does not accept his gifts.*

1.   Hear, my people, and take in the words of my lips.
2.   If anyone bring any gifts to an earthly ruler, and have dis-
     loyal thoughts in his heart, and the ruler know this, will
     he not be angry with him, and not refuse his gifts, and not
     give him over to judgement?
3.   Or if one man make himself appear good to another by
     deceit of tongue, but have evil in his heart, then will not
     the other understand the treachery of his heart, and himself
     be condemned, since his untruth was plain to all?
4.   And when the Lord shall send a great light, then there will
     be judgement for the just and the unjust, and there no one
     shall escape notice.

XLVII.

*Enoch instructs his sons from God's lips, and hands
them the handwriting of this book.*

1.   And now, my children, lay thought on your hearts, mark
     well the words of your father, which are all come to you
     from the Lord's lips.
2.   Take these books of your father's handwriting and read
     them.
3.   For the books are many, and in them you will learn all the
     Lord's works, all that has been from the beginning of cre-
     ation, and will be till the end of time.
4.   And if you will observe my handwriting, you will not sin
     against the Lord; because there is no other except the Lord,
     neither in heaven, nor in earth, nor in the very lowest
     places, nor in the one foundation.
5.   The Lord has placed the foundations in the unknown, and
     has spread forth heavens visible and invisible; he fixed the

earth on the waters, and created countless creatures, and who has counted the water and the foundation of the unfixed, or the dust of the earth, or the sand of the sea, or the drops of the rain, or the morning dew, or the wind's breathings? Who has filled earth and sea, and the indissoluble winter?

6. I cut the stars out of fire, and decorated heaven, and put it in their midst.

XLVIII.
Of the sun's passage along the seven circles.

1. That the sun go along the seven heavenly circles, which are the, appointment of one hundred and eighty-two thrones, that it go down on a short day, and again one hundred and eighty-two, that it go down on a big day, and he has two thrones on which he rests, revolving hither and thither above the thrones of the months, from the seventeenth day of the month Tsivan it goes down to the month Thevan, from the seventeenth of Thevan it goes up.

2. And thus it goes close to the earth, then the earth is and makes grow its fruit, and when it goes away, then the earth is sad, and trees and all fruits have no florescence.

3. All this he measured, with good measurement of hours, and fixed a measure by his wisdom, of the visible and the invisible.

4. From the invisible he made all things visible, Himself being invisible.

5. Thus I make known to you, my children, and distribute the books to your children, into all your generations, and amongst the nations who shall have the sense to fear God, let them receive them, and may they come to love them more than any food or earthly sweets, and read them and apply themselves to them.

6. And those who understand not the Lord, who fear not God, who accept not, but reject, who do not receive them (sc. the books), a terrible judgement awaits these.

7.   Blessed is the man who shall bear their yoke and shall drag them along, for he shall be released on the day of the great judgement.

XLIX.
Enoch instructs his sons not to swear either by
heaven or earth, and shows God's promise,
even in the mother's womb.

1.   I swear to you, my children, but I swear not by any oath, neither by heaven nor by earth, nor by any other creature which God created.
2.   The Lord said: "There is no oath in me, nor injustice, but truth."
3.   If there is no truth in men, let them swear by the words "yea, yea," or else, "nay, nay!"
4.   And I swear to you, yea, yea, that there has been no man in his mother's womb, but that already before, even to each one there is a place prepared for the repose of the soul, and a measure fixed how much it is intended that a man be tried in this world.
5.   Yea, children, deceive not yourselves, for there has been previously prepared a place for every soul of man.

L.
Of how none born on earth can remain hidden nor his work
remain concealed, but he (sc. God) bids us be meek,
to endure attack and insult, and not to offend widows and orphans.

1.   I have put everyman's work in writing and none born on earth can remain hidden nor his works remain concealed.
2.   I see all things.
3.   Now therefore, my children, in patience and meekness spend the number of your days, that you inherit endless life.
4.   Endure for the sake of the Lord every wound, every injury, every evil word and attack.

5. If ill-requitals befall you, return them not either to neigh-bour or enemy, because the Lord will return them for you and be your avenger on the day of great judgement, that there be no avenging here among men.
6. Whoever of you spends gold or silver for his brother's sake, he will receive ample treasure in the world to come.
7. Injure not widows nor orphans nor strangers, lest God's wrath come upon you.

LI.
Enoch instructs his sons, that they hide not treasures in the earth, but bids them give alms to the poor.

1. Stretch out your hands to the poor according to your strength.
2. Hide not your silver in the earth.
3. Help the faithful man in affliction, and affliction will not find you in the time of your trouble.
4. And every grievous and cruel yoke that come upon you bear all for the sake of the Lord, and thus you will find your reward in the day of judgement.
5. It is good to go morning, midday, and evening into the Lord's dwelling, for the glory of your creator.
6. Because every breathing thing glorifies Him, and every creature visible and invisible returns Him praise.

LII.
God instructs His faithful how they are to praise His name.

1. Blessed is the man who opens his lips in praise of God of Sabaoth and praises the Lord with his heart.
2. Cursed every man who opens his lips for the bringing into contempt and calumny of his neighbour, because he brings God into contempt.
3. Blessed is he who opens his lips blessing and praising God.
4. Cursed is he before the Lord all the days of his life, who opens his lips to curse and abuse.

5.   Blessed is he who blesses all the Lord's works.
6.   Cursed is he who brings the Lord's creation into contempt.
7.   Blessed is he who looks down and raises the fallen.
8.   Cursed is he who looks to and is eager for the destruction of what is not his.
9.   Blessed is he who keeps the foundations of his fathers made firm from the beginning.
10. Cursed is he who perverts the decrees of his forefathers.
11. Blessed is he who implants peace and love.
12. Cursed is he who disturbs those that love their neighbours.
13. Blessed is he who speaks with humble tongue and heart to all.
14. Cursed is he who speaks peace with his tongue, while in his heart there is no peace but a sword.
15. For all these things will be laid bare in the weighing-scales and in the books, on the day of the great judgement.

LIII.

*Let us not say: Our father is before God, he will stand
forward for us on the day of judgement,
for their father cannot help son, nor yet son father.*

1.   And now, my children, do not say: "Our father is standing before God, and is praying for our sins," for there is there no helper of any man who has sinned.
2.   You see how I wrote all works of every man, before his creation, all that is done amongst all men for all time, and none can tell or relate my handwriting, because the Lord sees all the imaginings of man, how they are vain, where they lie in the treasure-houses of the heart.
3.   And now, my children, mark well all the words of your father, that I tell you, lest you regret, saying: "Why did our father not tell us?"

LV.

Here Enoch shows his sons, telling them with tears: My children, the hour has approached for me to go up on to heaven; behold, the angels are standing before me.'

1. My children, behold, the day of my term and the time have approached.
2. For the angels who shall go with me are standing before me and urge me to my departure from you; they are standing here on earth, awaiting what has been told them.
3. For tomorrow I shall go up on to heaven, to the uppermost Jerusalem to my eternal inheritance.
4. Therefore, I bid you do before the Lord's face all his good pleasure.

LVI.

Methosalam asks of his father blessing, that he may make him food to eat.

1. Methosalam having answered his father Enoch, said: 'What is agreeable to thy eyes, father, that I may make before thy face, that thou mayst bless our dwellings, and thy sons, and that thy people may be made glorious through thee, and then that thou mayst depart thus, as the Lord said?
2. Enoch answered to his son Methosalam and said: "Hear, child, from the time when the Lord anointed me with the ointment of His glory, there has been no food in me, and my soul remembers not earthly enjoyment, neither do I want anything earthly!"

LVII.

Enoch bade his son Methosalam to summon all his brethren.

1. My child Methosalam, summon all thy brethren and our household and the elders of the people, that I may talk to them and depart, as is planned for me.

2. And Methosalam made haste, and summoned his brethren, Regim, Riman, Uchan, Chermion, Gaidad, and all the elders of the people before the face of his father Enoch; and he blessed them, and said to them:

LVIII.
Enoch's instruction to his sons.

1. Listen to me, my children, today.
2. In those days when the Lord came down on to earth for Adam's sake, and visited all his creatures, which he created himself, after all these he created Adam, and the Lord called all the beasts of the earth, all the reptiles, and all the birds that soar in the air, and brought them all before the face of our father Adam.
3. And Adam gave the names to all things living on earth.
4. And the Lord appointed him ruler over all, and subjected to him all things under his hands, and made them dumb and made them dull that they be commanded of man, and be in subjection and obedience to him.
5. Thus also the Lord created every man lord over all his possessions.
6. The Lord will not judge a single soul of beast for man's sake, but adjudges the souls of men to their beasts in this world; for men have a special place.
7. And as every soul of man is according to number, similarly beasts will not perish, nor all souls of beasts which the Lord created, till the great judgement, and they will accuse man, if he feed them ill.

LIX.
Enoch instructs his sons wherefore they may not
touch beef because of what comes from it.

1. Whoever defiles the soul of beasts, defiles his own soul.
2. For man brings clean animals to make sacrifice for sin, that he may have cure of his soul.

3. And if they bring for sacrifice clean animals, and birds, man has cure, he cures his soul.

4. All is given you for food, bind it by the four feet, that is to make good the cure, he cures his soul.

5. But whoever kills beast without wounds, kills his own soul and defiles his own flesh.

6. And he who does any beast any injury whatsoever, in secret, it is evil practice, and he defiles his own soul.

LX.

He who does injury to soul of man, does injury to his
own soul, and there is no cure for his flesh,
nor pardon for all time. How it is not fitting to kill
man neither by weapon nor by tongue.

1. He who works the killing of a man's soul, kills his own soul, and kills his own body, and there is no cure for him for all time.

2. He who puts a man in any snare, shall stick in it himself, and there is no cure for him for all time.

3. He who puts a man in any vessel, his retribution will not be wanting at the great judgement for all time.

4. He who works crookedly or speaks evil against any soul, will not make justice for himself for all time.

LXI.

Enoch instructs his sons to keep themselves from injustice
and often to stretch forth hands to the poor,
to give a share of their labours.

1. And now, my children, keep your hearts from every injustice, which the Lord hates. Just as a man asks (sc. something) for his own soul from God, so let him do to every living soul, because I know all things, how in the great time (sc. to come) are many mansions prepared for men, good for the good, and bad for the bad, without number many.

2. Blessed are those who enter the good houses, for in the bad (sc. houses) there is no peace nor return (sc. from them).
3. Hear, my children, small and great! When man puts a good thought in his heart, brings gifts from his labours before the Lord's face and his hands made them not, then the Lord will turn away his face from the labour of his hand, and he (sc. man) cannot find the labour of his hands.
4. And if his hands made it, but his heart murmur, and his heart cease not making murmur incessantly, he has not any advantage.

LXII.

Of how it is fitting to bring ones gift with faith,
because there is no repentance after death.

1. Blessed is the man who in his patience brings his gifts with faith before the Lord's face, because he will find forgiveness of sins.
2. But if he take back his words before the time, there is no repentance for him; and if the time pass and he do not of his own will what is promised, there is no repentance after death.
3. Because every work which man does before the time, is all deceit before men, and sin before God.

LXIII.

Of how not to despise the pool; but to share with them
equally, lest thou be murmured against before God.

1. When man clothes the naked and fills the hungry, he will find reward from God.
2. But if his heart murmur, he commits a double evil: ruin of himself and of that which he gives; and for him there will be no finding of reward on account of that.
3. And if his own heart is filled with his food and his own flesh (sc. clothed) with his clothing he commits contempt,

and forfeit all his endurance of poverty, and will not find reward of his good deeds.

4.   Every proud and magniloquent man is hateful to the Lord, and every false speech, clothed in untruth; it will be cut with the blade of the sword of death, and thrown into the fire, and shall burn for all time.'

XLIV.
Of how the Lord calls up Enoch, and people took counsel to go and kiss him at the place called Achuzan.

1.   When Enoch had spoken these words to his sons, all people far and near heard how the Lord was calling Enoch. They took counsel together:

2.   "Let us go and kiss Enoch" and two thousand men came together and came to the place Achuzan where Enoch was, and his sons.

3.   And the elders of the people, the whole assembly, came and bowed down and began to kiss Enoch and said to him:

4.   "Our father Enoch, be thou blessed of the Lord, the eternal ruler, and now bless thy sons and all the people, that we may be glorified today before thy face.

5.   For thou shalt be glorified before the Lord's face for all time, since the Lord chose thee, rather than all men on earth, and designated thee writer of all his creation, visible and invisible, and redeemer of the sins of man, and helper of thy household."

LXV.
Of Enoch's instruction of his sons.

1.   And Enoch answered all his people saying: 'Hear, my children, before that all creatures were created, the Lord created the visible and invisible things.

2.   And as much time as there was and went past, understand that after that he created man in the likeness of his own

form, and put into him eyes to see, and ears to hear, and heart to reflect, and intellect wherewith to deliberate.

3. And the Lord saw all man's works, and created all his creatures, and divided time, from time he fixed the years, and from the years he appointed the months, and from the months he appointed the days, and of days he appointed seven.

4. And in those he appointed the hours, measured them out exactly, that man might reflect on time and count years, months, and hours, their alternation, beginning, and end, and that he might count his own life, from the beginning until death, and reflect on his sin and write his work bad and good; because no work is hidden before the Lord, that every man might know his works and never transgress all his commandments, and keep my handwriting from generation to generation.

5. When all creation visible and invisible, as the Lord created it, shall end, then every man goes to the great judgement, and then all time shall perish, and the years, and thenceforward there will be neither months nor days nor hours, they will be stuck together and will not be counted.

6. There will be one aeon, and all the righteous who shall escape the Lord's great judgement, shall be collected in the great aeon, for the righteous the great aeon will begin, and they will live eternally, and then too there will be amongst them neither labour, nor sickness, nor humiliation, nor anxiety, nor need, nor violence, nor night, nor darkness, but great light.

7. And they shall have a great indestructible wall, and a paradise bright and incorruptible, for all corruptible things shall pass away, and there will be eternal life

LXVI.

*Enoch instructs his sons and all the elders of the
people, how they are to walk with terror
and trembling before the Lord, and serve Him alone
and not bow down to idols, but to God,
who created heaven and earth and every creature, and to His image.*

1. And now, my children, keep your souls from all injustice, such as the Lord hates.
2. Walk before His face with terror and trembling and serve Him alone.
3. Bow down to the true God, not to dumb idols, but bow down to His picture, and bring all just offerings before the Lord's face. The Lord hates what is unjust.
4. For the Lord sees all things; when man takes thought in his heart, then he counsels the intellects, and every thought is always before the Lord, who made firm the earth and put all creatures on it.
5. If you look to heaven, the Lord is there; if you take thought of the sea's deep and all the underearth, the Lord is there.
6. For the Lord created all things. Bow not down to things made by man, leaving the Lord of all creation, because no work can remain hidden before the Lord's face.
7. Walk, my children, in longsuffering, in meekness, honesty, in provocation, in grief, in faith and in truth, in reliance on promises, in illness, in abuse, in wounds, in temptation, in nakedness, in privation, loving one another, till you go out from this age of ills, that you become inheritors of endless time.
8. Blessed are the just who shall escape the great judgement, for they shall shine forth more than the sun sevenfold, for in this world the seventh part is taken off from all, light, darkness, food, enjoyment, sorrow, paradise, torture, fire, frost, and other things; he put all down in writing, that you might read and understand.'

LXVII.

*The Lord let out darkness on to earth and covered the
people and Enoch, and he was taken up on high,
and light came again in the heaven.*

1. When Enoch had talked to the people, the Lord sent out darkness on to the earth, and there was darkness, and it covered those men standing with Enoch, and they took Enoch up on to the highest heaven, where the Lord is; and he received him and placed him before his face, and the darkness went off from the earth, and light came again.

2. And the people saw and understood not how Enoch had been taken, and glorified God, and found a roll in which was traced 'the invisible God'; and all went to their homes.

LXVIII.

1. Enoch was born on the sixth day of the month Tsivan, and lived three hundred and sixty-five years.

2. He was taken up to heaven on the first day of the month Tsivan and remained in heaven sixty days.

3. He wrote all these signs of all creation, which the Lord created, and wrote three hundred and sixty-six books, and handed them over to his sons and remained on earth thirty days, and was again taken up to heaven on the sixth day of the month Tsivan, on the very day and hour when he was born.

4. As every man's nature in this life is dark, so are also his conception, birth, and departure from this life.

5. At what hour he was conceived, at that hour he was born, and at that hour too he died.

6. Methosalam and his brethren, all the sons of Enoch, made haste, and erected an altar at the place called Achuzan, whence and where Enoch had been taken up to heaven.

7. And they took sacrificial oxen and summoned all people and sacrificed the sacrifice before the Lord's face.

8. All people, the elders of the people and the whole assembly came to the feast and brought gifts to the sons of Enoch.

9. And they made a great feast, rejoicing and making merry three days, praising God, who had given them such a sign through Enoch, who had found favour with Him, and that they should hand it on to their sons from generation to generation, from age to age.

10. Amen.

The Grace of God
A poem by Sis. Halima

It is the grace of God that I can be here
To speak of His wondrous works
It is the grace of God that I have no fear
When I know the enemy lurks
It is his grace I say that I am aware
Of the things I cannot see
Now that I see the grace of my precious Lord
I know I have victory
It is the grace of God that I do believe
That He gave a gift to me
Christ is the one who said:
"whosoever will come…", they will have eternity
It is His grace I say that lets me endure
The ups and downs of life
He lets me see that there's an ultimate price
And Christ made that sacrifice
It is the grace of God that lets me have joy
Although my enemies fight
I know within their hearts, they want us to fail
But the Lord is our strength and might
It is His grace I say that lets us become
A child of the true living God
Now that I AM his child I know for sure
No matter what, I will survive.

Let us therefore come boldly unto the throne
of grace, that we may obtain mercy
And find grace to help in time of need.
—Hebrews 4:16

Then said one unto Him, Lord, are there *few that may be saved?* And He said unto them, Strive to enter in at the strait (narrow) gate: for many, I say unto you, will seek to enter in (when He comes), and shall not be able, when once the "Master of the House" is risen up, and hath *shut the door,* and ye begin to stand without, and to knock at the door, saying, Lord, open unto us: and He shall answer and say unto you, *I know not whence ye are:* then shall ye begin to say, We have eaten and drunk in Thy presence, and Thou hast taught in our streets. But He shall say, I tell you, I know you not whence ye are; depart from me, all ye workers of iniquity. *(Luke 13:23–27)*

5

The Book of Revelation

Although I Suffer
A poem by Sis. Halima

Although I suffer
My Lord, He's there
Although I suffer
I know he cares
There's times I cry out
I moan and groan
Then I hear my Lord say
There's no more tears when you get home
Although I suffer
In pain all night long
My soul it rejoiceth
And sings a beautiful song
I know He'll never leave me
Nor forsake me its true
I know He'll stand by me
Hey, He'll stand by you too
Although I suffer
I look forward to the day
When I see my Lord Jesus
Wipe all my pain away

*And God shall wipe away all tears from their eyes
and there shall be no more death neither sorrow
Nor crying neither shall there be anymore
pain For the former things are passed away.*
—Revelation 21:4

Behold I Show You a Mystery

Some claim that "all" the Church are to pass through the Tribulation; others that "all" the Church are to be caught out before the Tribulation, while some claim that only the "waiting" and "Watching" Saints shall be caught out before the Tribulation, and that the rest must pass through it.

The latter base their claim on Hebrews 9:28, where it says: "Unto them that look for Him shall he appear the second time without sin unto salvation." While this might apply to the living when He appears, it certainly cannot apply to the dead.

There are ten and hundreds of thousands who "fell asleep in Jesus" who never heard of the Pre-millennial Coming of the Lord, or at least never grasped its meaning, and who therefore never "watched" and "waited" and "looked" for His Appearing.

They surely are "In Christ"; and the "Dead in Christ" are to rise at the Rapture. Paul does not say in 1 Thessalonians 4:16–17 that it will be the "dead" who "watched" and "waited" and "looked," and those who are "alive" and "watch" and "wait" and "look" for His Appearing that shall be "caught out," but the dead "in Christ, "and we who "are alive and remain."

The order of the Resurrection is—"Christ the 'First Fruits,' afterward they that 'are Christ's at His Coming." Paul says, "Behold I show you a mystery; we shall not all 'sleep,' but we shall *all* be changed" (1 Cor. 15:51).

Then there is another fact that we must not forget, and that is, the Unity of the Church.

"For as the Body is One, and hath many members, and *all* the Members of That One Body, Being Many *are one body*; so also is Christ. For by One Spirit are we *all* Baptized into One Body" (1 Cor. 12:12–13).

All then who have been "born again" (John 3:3–7) are part of Christ's "Body," and we cannot conceive of Christ's "Body" being divided; part of it remaining "asleep" in the grave and part of it "raised in glory"; part of it left to pass through the Tribulation, and part of it "changed" and caught up to meet Him in the air.

If "all" the Church are to pass through the Tribulation, then instead of waiting and watching "for the Lord," we should be waiting and watching "for the Tribulation," which is contrary to the teaching of Christ Himself (Matt. 24:42–44).

The Tribulation is not for the perfecting "of the Saints." It has nothing to do with the Church. It is the time of "Jacob's Trouble" (Jer. 30:7), and is the "Judgment of Israel," and it is God's purpose to keep the Church out of it (Rev. 2:10).

The Book of Revelation is written in chronological order. After the fourth chapter, the Church is seen no more upon the earth until she appears in the nineteenth chapter coming with the Bridegroom "from" Heaven.

The entire time between these two chapters is filled with appalling judgments that fall upon those who "dwell on the earth," and as the Church is not of the earth, but is supposed to "sit together in 'Heavenly Places' in Christ Jesus" (Eph. 2:6). She will not be among those who "dwell on the earth" in those days.

The confusion is largely due to the fact that students of prophetic truth do not distinguish between Christ's coming *for* His Saints, and *with* His Saints. The former is called the "Rapture," the latter the "Revelation."

Numerous passages in scripture *speak of* Christ coming "with" His Saints (Zech. 14:5, Col. 3:4, 1 Thess. 3:13, 1 Thess. 4:14, Jude 14), but it is evident that they cannot come "with" Him, if they had not been previously caught out "to" Him.

All such passages refer therefore to the "Revelation" and not the "Rapture."

The typical teaching of the Scriptures demand that the Church be caught out "before" the Tribulation. Joseph was a type of Christ, and he was espoused to, and married Asenath, a Gentile bride, during the time of his "rejection by his brethren," and "before the famine," which typified the Tribulation, because it was the time of "Judgment of his Brethren."

This is the time of Christ's rejection by "His Brethren"—the Jews, and to complete the type He must get His Bride—the church "before" the Tribulation.

Moses, who is also a type of Christ, got his bride, and she a Gentile, "after" his rejection by his brethren, and "before" they passed through the Tribulation under Pharaoh. (Exod. 2:23–25).

Enoch, a type of the "Translation Saints," was caught out "before" the Flood, and Flood is a type of the Tribulation, and Noah and his family of the "Jewish Remnant" or 144,000 sealed ones of Rev. 7:1–8, who will be preserved through the Tribulation.

How thrilling the thought that some of us shall not die, that in a moment, in the "twinkling of an eye" without being unclothed by the ghastly hands of death, and instead of the winding sheet of the grave, we shall be instantly changed and clothed with the glorious garments of immortality.

What a transport of joy will fill our being as we suddenly feel the thrill of immortality throbbing through our veins and find ourselves being transported through the air in the company of fellow Christians and of our loved ones who fell asleep in Jesus.

What welcome recognitions and greetings there will be as we journey up with them to the "Bridal Halls of Heaven," where we shall join in the new and triumphal song of Moses and the Lamb (Rev. 5:9–10).

Revelation 1

1. The Revelation of Jesus Christ, which God gave unto him, to shew unto his servants things which must shortly come to pass; and he sent and signified it by his angel unto his servant John.
2. Who bare record of the word of God, and of the testimony of Jesus Christ, and of all things that he saw.
3. Blessed is he that readeth, and they that hear the words of this prophecy, and keep those things which are written therein: for the time is at hand.
4. John to the seven churches which are in Asia: Grace be unto you, and peace, from him which is, and which was, and which is to come; and from the seven Spirits which are before his throne.

5. And from Jesus Christ, who is the faithful witness, and the first begotten of the dead, and the prince of the kings of the earth. Unto him that loved us, and washed us from our sins in his own blood.

6. And hath made us kings and priests unto God and his Father; to him be glory and dominion for ever and ever. Amen.

7. Behold, he cometh with clouds; and every eye shall see him, and they also which pierced him: and all kindreds of the earth shall wail because of him. Even so, Amen.

8. I am Alpha and Omega, the beginning and the ending, saith the Lord, which is, and which was, and which is to come, the Almighty.

9. I, John, who also am your brother, and companion in tribulation, and in the kingdom and patience of Jesus Christ, was in the isle that is called Patmos, for the word of God, and for the testimony of Jesus Christ.

10. I was in the Spirit on the Lord's day, and heard behind me a great voice, as of a trumpet.

11. Saying, I am Alpha and Omega, the first and the last: and, What thou seest, write in a book, and send it unto the seven churches which are in Asia; unto Ephesus, and unto Smyrna, and unto Pergamos, and unto Thyatira, and unto Sardis, and unto Philadelphia, and unto Laodicea.

12. And I turned to see the voice that spake with me. And being turned, I saw seven golden candlesticks.

13. And in the midst of the seven candlesticks one like unto the Son of man, clothed with a garment down to the foot, and girt about the paps with a golden girdle.

14. His head and his hairs were white like wool, as white as snow; and his eyes were as a flame of fire.

15. And his feet like unto fine brass, as if they burned in a furnace; and his voice as the sound of many waters.

16. And he had in his right hand seven stars: and out of his mouth went a sharp two-edged sword: and his countenance was as the sun shineth in his strength.

17. And when I saw him, I fell at his feet as dead. And he laid his right hand upon me, saying unto me, Fear not; I am the first and the last.
18. I am he that liveth, and was dead; and, behold, I am alive for evermore, Amen; and have the keys of hell and of death.
19. Write the things which thou hast seen, and the things which are, and the things which shall be hereafter.
20. The mystery of the seven stars which thou sawest in my right hand, and the seven golden candlesticks. The seven stars are the angels of the seven churches: and the seven candlesticks which thou sawest are the seven churches.

Revelation 2

1. Unto the angel of the church of Ephesus write; These things saith he that holdeth the seven stars in his right hand, who walketh in the midst of the seven golden candlesticks.
2. I know thy works, and thy labour, and thy patience, and how thou canst not bear them which are evil: and thou hast tried them which say they are apostles, and are not, and hast found them liars.
3. And hast borne, and hast patience, and for my name's sake hast laboured, and hast not fainted.
4. Nevertheless I have somewhat against thee, because thou hast left thy first love.
5. Remember therefore from whence thou art fallen, and repent, and do the first works; or else I will come unto thee quickly, and will remove thy candlestick out of his place, except thou repent.
6. But this thou hast, that thou hatest the deeds of the Nicolaitanes, which I also hate.
7. He that hath an ear, let him hear what the Spirit saith unto the churches; To him that overcometh will I give to eat of the tree of life, which is in the midst of the paradise of God.
8. And unto the angel of the church in Smyrna write; These things saith the first and the last, which was dead, and is alive.

9. I know thy works, and tribulation, and poverty, (but thou art rich) and I know the blasphemy of them which say they are Jews, and are not, but are the synagogue of Satan.

10. Fear none of those things which thou shalt suffer: behold, the devil shall cast some of you into prison, that ye may be tried; and ye shall have tribulation ten days: be thou faithful unto death, and I will give thee a crown of life.

11. He that hath an ear, let him hear what the Spirit saith unto the churches; He that overcometh shall not be hurt of the second death.

12. And to the angel of the church in Pergamos write; These things saith he which hath the sharp sword with two edges.

13. I know thy works, and where thou dwellest, even where Satan's seat is: and thou holdest fast my name, and hast not denied my faith, even in those days wherein Antipas was my faithful martyr, who was slain among you, where Satan dwelleth.

14. But I have a few things against thee, because thou hast there them that hold the doctrine of Balaam, who taught Balac to cast a stumbling block before the children of Israel, to eat things sacrificed unto idols, and to commit fornication.

15. So hast thou also them that hold the doctrine of the Nicolaitanes, which thing I hate.

16. Repent; or else I will come unto thee quickly, and will fight against them with the sword of my mouth.

17. He that hath an ear, let him hear what the Spirit saith unto the churches; To him that overcometh will I give to eat of the hidden manna, and will give him a white stone, and in the stone a new name written, which no man knoweth saving he that receiveth it.

18. And unto the angel of the church in Thyatira write; These things saith the Son of God, who hath his eyes like unto a flame of fire, and his feet are like fine brass.

19. I know thy works, and charity, and service, and faith, and thy patience, and thy works; and the last to be more than the first.

20. Notwithstanding I have a few things against thee, because thou sufferest that woman Jezebel, which calleth herself a prophetess, to teach and to seduce my servants to commit fornication, and to eat things sacrificed unto idols.

21. And I gave her space to repent of her fornication; and she repented not.

22. Behold, I will cast her into a bed, and them that commit adultery with her into great tribulation, except they repent of their deeds.

23. And I will kill her children with death; and all the churches shall know that I am he which searcheth the reins and hearts: and I will give unto every one of you according to your works.

24. But unto you I say, and unto the rest in Thyatira, as many as have not this doctrine, and which have not known the depths of Satan, as they speak; I will put upon you none other burden.

25. But that which ye have already hold fast till I come.

26. And he that overcometh, and keepeth my works unto the end, to him will I give power over the nations:

27. And he shall rule them with a rod of iron; as the vessels of a potter shall they be broken to shivers: even as I received of my Father.

28. And I will give him the morning star.

29. He that hath an ear, let him hear what the Spirit saith unto the churches.

Revelation 3

1. And unto the angel of the church in Sardis write; These things saith he that hath the seven Spirits of God, and the seven stars; I know thy works, that thou hast a name that thou livest, and art dead.

2. Be watchful, and strengthen the things which remain, that are ready to die: for I have not found thy works perfect before God.

3. Remember therefore how thou hast received and heard, and hold fast, and repent. If therefore thou shalt not watch, I will come on thee as a thief, and thou shalt not know what hour I will come upon thee.

4. Thou hast a few names even in Sardis which have not defiled their garments; and they shall walk with me in white: for they are worthy.

5. He that overcometh, the same shall be clothed in white raiment; and I will not blot out his name out of the book of life, but I will confess his name before my Father, and before his angels.

6. He that hath an ear, let him hear what the Spirit saith unto the churches.

7. And to the angel of the church in Philadelphia write; These things saith he that is holy, he that is true, he that hath the key of David, he that openeth, and no man shutteth; and shutteth, and no man openeth.

8. I know thy works: behold, I have set before thee an open door, and no man can shut it: for thou hast a little strength, and hast kept my word, and hast not denied my name.

9. Behold, I will make them of the synagogue of Satan, which say they are Jews, and are not, but do lie; behold, I will make them to come and worship before thy feet, and to know that I have loved thee.

10. Because thou hast kept the word of my patience, I also will keep thee from the hour of temptation, which shall come upon all the world, to try them that dwell upon the earth.

11. Behold, I come quickly: hold that fast which thou hast, that no man take thy crown.

12. Him that overcometh will I make a pillar in the temple of my God, and he shall go no more out: and I will write upon him the name of my God, and the name of the city of my God, which is new Jerusalem, which cometh down out of heaven from my God: and I will write upon him my new name.

13. He that hath an ear, let him hear what the Spirit saith unto the churches.

14. And unto the angel of the church of the Laodiceans write; These things saith the Amen, the faithful and true witness, the beginning of the creation of God.

15. I know thy works, that thou art neither cold nor hot: I would thou wert cold or hot.

16. So then because thou art lukewarm, and neither cold nor hot, I will spew thee out of my mouth.

17. Because thou sayest, I am rich, and increased with goods, and have need of nothing; and knowest not that thou art wretched, and miserable, and poor, and blind, and naked.

18. I counsel thee to buy of me gold tried in the fire, that thou mayest be rich; and white raiment, that thou mayest be clothed, and that the shame of thy nakedness do not appear; and anoint thine eyes with eye salve, that thou mayest see.

19. As many as I love, I rebuke and chasten: be zealous therefore, and repent.

20. Behold, I stand at the door, and knock: if any man hear my voice, and open the door, I will come in to him, and will sup with him, and he with me.

21. To him that overcometh will I grant to sit with me in my throne, even as I also overcame, and am set down with my Father in his throne.

22. He that hath an ear, let him hear what the Spirit saith unto the churches.

Revelation 4

1. After this I looked, and, behold, a door was opened in heaven: and the first voice which I heard was as it were of a trumpet talking with me; which said, Come up hither, and I will shew thee things which must be hereafter.

2. And immediately I was in the spirit: and, behold, a throne was set in heaven, and one sat on the throne.

3. And he that sat was to look upon like a jasper and a sardine stone: and there was a rainbow round about the throne, in sight like unto an emerald.

4. And round about the throne were four and twenty seats: and upon the seats I saw four and twenty elders sitting, clothed in white raiment; and they had on their heads crowns of gold.

5. And out of the throne proceeded lightnings and thunderings and voices: and there were seven lamps of fire burning before the throne, which are the seven Spirits of God.

6. And before the throne there was a sea of glass like unto crystal: and in the midst of the throne, and round about the throne, were four beasts full of eyes before and behind.

7. And the first beast was like a lion, and the second beast like a calf, and the third beast had a face as a man, and the fourth beast was like a flying eagle.

8. And the four beasts had each of them six wings about him; and they were full of eyes within: and they rest not day and night, saying, Holy, holy, holy, LORD God Almighty, which was, and is, and is to come.

9. And when those beasts give glory and honour and thanks to him that sat on the throne, who liveth for ever and ever,

10. The four and twenty elders fall down before him that sat on the throne, and worship him that liveth for ever and ever, and cast their crowns before the throne, saying,

11. Thou art worthy, O Lord, to receive glory and honour and power: for thou hast created all things, and for thy pleasure they are and were created.

Revelation 5

1. And I saw in the right hand of him that sat on the throne a book written within and on the backside, sealed with seven seals.

2. And I saw a strong angel proclaiming with a loud voice, Who is worthy to open the book and to loose the seals thereof?

3. And no man in heaven, nor in earth, neither under the earth, was able to open the book, neither to look thereon.

4. And I wept much, because no man was found worthy to open and to read the book, neither to look thereon.

5. And one of the elders saith unto me, Weep not: behold, the Lion of the tribe of Judah, the Root of David, hath prevailed to open the book, and to loose the seven seals thereof.

6. And I beheld, and, lo, in the midst of the throne and of the four beasts, and in the midst of the elders, stood a Lamb as it had been slain, having seven horns and seven eyes, which are the seven Spirits of God sent forth into all the earth.

7. And he came and took the book out of the right hand of him that sat upon the throne.

8. And when he had taken the book, the four beasts and four and twenty elders fell down before the Lamb, having every one of them harps, and golden vials full of odours, which are the prayers of saints.

9. And they sung a new song, saying, Thou art worthy to take the book, and to open the seals thereof: for thou wast slain, and hast redeemed us to God by thy blood out of every kindred, and tongue, and people, and nation.

10. And hast made us unto our God kings and priests: and we shall reign on the earth.

11. And I beheld, and I heard the voice of many angels round about the throne and the beasts and the elders: and the number of them was ten thousand times ten thousand, and thousands of thousands.

12. Saying with a loud voice, Worthy is the Lamb that was slain to receive power, and riches, and wisdom, and strength, and honour, and glory, and blessing.

13. And every creature which is in heaven, and on the earth, and under the earth, and such as are in the sea, and all that are in them, heard I saying, Blessing, and honour, and glory, and power, be unto him that sitteth upon the throne, and unto the Lamb for ever and ever.

14. And the four beasts said, Amen. And the four and twenty elders fell down and worshipped him that liveth for ever and ever.

Revelation 6

1. And I saw when the Lamb opened one of the seals, and I heard, as it were the noise of thunder, one of the four beasts saying, Come and see.
2. And I saw, and behold a white horse: and he that sat on him had a bow; and a crown was given unto him: and he went forth conquering, and to conquer.
3. And when he had opened the second seal, I heard the second beast say, Come and see.
4. And there went out another horse that was red: and power was given to him that sat thereon to take peace from the earth, and that they should kill one another: and there was given unto him a great sword.
5. And when he had opened the third seal, I heard the third beast say, Come and see. And I beheld, and lo a black horse; and he that sat on him had a pair of balances in his hand.
6. And I heard a voice in the midst of the four beasts say, A measure of wheat for a penny, and three measures of barley for a penny; and see thou hurt not the oil and the wine.
7. And when he had opened the fourth seal, I heard the voice of the fourth beast say, Come and see.
8. And I looked, and behold a pale horse: and his name that sat on him was Death, and Hell followed with him. And power was given unto them over the fourth part of the earth, to kill with sword, and with hunger, and with death, and with the beasts of the earth.
9. And when he had opened the fifth seal, I saw under the altar the souls of them that were slain for the word of God, and for the testimony which they held.
10. And they cried with a loud voice, saying, How long, O Lord, holy and true, dost thou not judge and avenge our blood on them that dwell on the earth?
11. And white robes were given unto every one of them; and it was said unto them, that they should rest yet for a little

season, until their fellow servants also and their brethren, that should be killed as they were, should be fulfilled.

12. And I beheld when he had opened the sixth seal, and, lo, there was a great earthquake; and the sun became black as sackcloth of hair, and the moon became as blood.

13. And the stars of heaven fell unto the earth, even as a fig tree casteth her untimely figs, when she is shaken of a mighty wind.

14. And the heaven departed as a scroll when it is rolled together; and every mountain and island were moved out of their places.

15. And the kings of the earth, and the great men, and the rich men, and the chief captains, and the mighty men, and every bondman, and every free man, hid themselves in the dens and in the rocks of the mountains.

16. And said to the mountains and rocks, Fall on us, and hide us from the face of him that sitteth on the throne, and from the wrath of the Lamb.

17. For the great day of his wrath is come; and who shall be able to stand?

Revelation 7

1. And after these things I saw four angels standing on the four comers of the earth, holding the four winds of the earth, that the wind should not blow on the earth, nor on the sea, nor on any tree.

2. And I saw another angel ascending from the east, having the seal of the living God: and he cried with a loud voice to the four angels, to whom it was given to hurt the earth and the sea,

3. Saying, Hurt not the earth, neither the sea, nor the trees, till we have sealed the servants of our God in their foreheads.

4. And I heard the number of them which were sealed: and there were sealed a hundred and forty and four thousand of all the tribes of the children of Israel.

5. Of the tribe of Judah were sealed twelve thousand. Of the tribe of Reuben were sealed twelve thousand. Of the tribe of Gad were sealed twelve thousand.

6. Of the tribe of Aser were sealed twelve thousand. Of the tribe of Nephthalim were sealed twelve thousand. Of the tribe of Manasses were sealed twelve thousand.

7. Of the tribe of Simeon were sealed twelve thousand. Of the tribe of Levi were sealed twelve thousand. Of the tribe of Issachar were sealed twelve thousand.

8. Of the tribe of Zabulon were sealed twelve thousand. Of the tribe of Joseph were sealed twelve thousand. Of the tribe of Benjamin were sealed twelve thousand.

9. After this I beheld, and, lo, a great multitude, which no man could number, of all nations, and kindreds, and people, and tongues, stood before the throne, and before the Lamb, clothed with white robes, and palms in their hands.

10. And cried with a loud voice, saying, Salvation to our God which sitteth upon the throne, and unto the Lamb.

11. And all the angels stood round about the throne, and about the elders and the four beasts, and fell before the throne on their faces, and worshipped God.

12. Saying, Amen: Blessing, and glory, and wisdom, and thanksgiving, and honour, and power, and might, be unto our God for ever and ever. Amen.

13. And one of the elders answered, saying unto me, What are these which are arrayed in white robes? and whence came they?

14. And I said unto him, Sir, thou knowest. And he said to me, These are they which came out of great tribulation, and have washed their robes, and made them white in the blood of the Lamb.

15. Therefore are they before the throne of God, and SGN8 him day and night in his temple: and he that sitteth on the throne shall dwell among them.

16. They shall hunger no more, neither thirst anymore; neither shall the sun light on them, nor any heat.

17. For the Lamb which is in the midst of the throne shall feed them, and shall lead them unto living fountains of waters: and God shall wipe away all tears from their eyes.

Revelation 8

1. And when he had opened the seventh seal, there was silence in heaven about the space of half an hour.
2. And I saw the seven angels which stood before God; and to them were given seven trumpets.
3. And another angel came and stood at the altar, having a golden censer; and there was given unto him much incense, that he should offer it with the prayers of all saints upon the golden altar which was before the throne.
4. And the smoke of the incense, which came with the prayers of the saints, ascended up before God out of the angel's hand.
5. And the angel took the censer, and filled it with fire of the altar, and cast it into the earth: and there were voices, and thunderings, and lightnings, and an earthquake.
6. And the seven angels which had the seven trumpets prepared themselves to sound.
7. The first angel sounded, and there followed hail and fire mingled with blood, and they were cast upon the earth: and the third part of trees was burnt up, and all green grass was burnt up.
8. And the second angel sounded, and as it were a great mountain burning with fire was cast into the sea: and the third part of the sea became blood.
9. And the third part of the creatures which were in the sea, and had life, died; and the third part of the ships were destroyed.
10. And the third angel sounded, and there fell a great star from heaven, burning as it were a lamp, and it fell upon the third part of the rivers, and upon the fountains of waters.
11. And the name of the star is called Wormwood: and the third part of the waters became wormwood; and many men died of the waters, because they were made bitter.

12. And the fourth angel sounded, and the third part of the sun was smitten, and the third part of the moon, and the third part of the stars; so as the third part of them was darkened, and the day shone not for a third part of it, and the night likewise.

13. And I beheld, and heard an angel flying through the midst of heaven, saying with a loud voice, Woe, woe, woe, to the inhabiters of the earth by reason of the other voices of the trumpet of the three angels, which are yet to sound!

Revelation 9

1. And the fifth angel sounded, and I saw a star fall from heaven unto the earth: and to him was given the key of the bottomless pit.

2. And he opened the bottomless pit; and there arose a smoke out of the pit, as the smoke of a great furnace; and the sun and the air were darkened by reason of the smoke of the pit.

3. And there came out of the smoke locusts upon the earth: and unto them was given power, as the scorpions of the earth have power.

4. And it was commanded them that they should not hurt the grass of the earth, neither any green thing, neither any tree; but only those men which have not the seal of God in their foreheads.

5. And to them it was given that they should not kill them, but that they should be tormented five months: and their torment was as the torment of a scorpion, when he striketh a man.

6. And in those days shall men seek death, and shall not find it; and shall desire to die, and death shall flee from them.

7. And the shapes of the locusts were like unto horses prepared unto battle; and on their heads were as it were crowns like gold, and their faces were as the faces of men.

8. And they had hair as the hair of women, and their teeth were as the teeth of lions.

9. And they had breastplates, as it were breastplates of iron; and the sound of their wings was as the sound of chariots of many horses running to battle.

10. And they had tails like unto scorpions, and there were stings in their tails: and their power was to hurt men five months.

11. And they had a king over them, which is the angel of the bottomless pit, whose name in the Hebrew tongue is Abaddon, but in the Greek tongue hath his name Apollyon.

12. One woe is past; and, behold, there come two woes more hereafter.

13. And the sixth angel sounded, and I heard a voice from the four horns of the golden altar which is before God.

14. Saying to the sixth angel which had the trumpet, Loose the four angels which are bound in the great river Euphrates.

15. And the four angels were loosed, which were prepared for an hour, and a day, and a month, and a year, for to slay the third part of men.

16. And the number of the army of the horsemen were two hundred thousand: and I heard the number of them.

17. And thus I saw the horses in the vision, and them that sat on them, having breastplates of fire, and of jacinth, and brimstone: and the heads of the horses were as the heads of lions; and out of their mouths issued fire and smoke and brimstone.

18. By these three was the third part of men killed, by the fire, and by the smoke, and by the brimstone, which issued out of their mouths.

19. For their power is in their mouth, and in their tails: for their tails were like unto serpents, and had heads, and with them they do hurt.

20. And the rest of the men which were not killed by these plagues yet repented not of the works of their hands, that they should not worship devils, and idols.

Revelation 10

1. And I saw another mighty angel come down from heaven, clothed with a cloud: and a rainbow was upon his head, and his face was as it were the sun, and his feet as pillars of fire.
2. And he had in his hand a little book open: and he set his right foot upon the sea, and his left foot on the earth.
3. And cried with a loud voice, as when a lion roareth: and when he had cried, seven thunders uttered their voices.
4. And when the seven thunders had uttered their voices, I was about to write: and I heard a voice from heaven saying unto me, Seal up those things which the seven thunders uttered, and write them not.
5. And the angel which I saw stand upon the sea and upon the earth lifted up his hand to heaven,
6. And sware by him that liveth for ever and ever, who created heaven, and the things that therein are, and the earth, and the things that therein are, and the sea, and the things which are therein, that there should be time no longer.
7. But in the days of the voice of the seventh angel, when he shall begin to sound, the mystery of God should be finished, as he hath declared to his servants the prophets.
8. And the voice which I heard from heaven spake unto me again, and said, Go and take the little book which is open in the hand of the angel which standeth upon the sea and upon the earth.
9. And I went unto the angel, and said unto him, Give me the little book. And he said unto me, Take it, and eat it up; and it shall make thy belly bitter, but it shall be in thy mouth sweet as honey.
10. And I took the little book out of the angel's hand, and ate it up; and it was in my mouth sweet as honey: and as soon as I had eaten it, my belly was bitter.
11. And he said unto me, Thou must prophesy again before many peoples, and nations, and tongues, and kings.

Revelation 11

1. And there was given me a reed like unto a rod: and the angel stood, saying, Rise, and measure the temple of God, and the altar, and them that worship therein.
2. But the court which is without the temple leave out, and measure it not; for it is given unto the Gentiles: and the holy city shall they tread under foot forty and two months.
3. And I will give power unto my two witnesses, and they shall prophesy a thousand two hundred and threescore days, clothed in sackcloth.
4. These are the two olive trees, and the two candlesticks standing before the God of the earth.
5. And if any man will hurt them, fire proceedeth out of their mouth, and devoureth their enemies: and if any man will hurt them, he must in this manner be killed.
6. These have power to shut heaven, that it rain not in the days of their prophecy: and have power over waters to turn them to blood, and to smite the earth with all plagues, as often as they will.
7. And when they shall have finished their testimony, the beast that ascendeth out of the bottomless pit shall make war against them, and shall overcome them, and kill them.
8. And their dead bodies shall lie in the street of the great city, which spiritually is called Sodom and Egypt, where also our Lord was crucified.
9. And they of the people and kindreds and tongues and nations shall see their dead bodies three days and a half, and shall not suffer their dead bodies to be put in graves.
10. And they that dwell upon the earth shall rejoice over them, and make merry, and shall send gifts one to another; because these two prophets tormented them that dwelt on the earth.
11. And after three days and a half the spirit of life from God entered into them, and they stood upon their feet; and great fear fell upon them which saw them.

12. And they heard a great voice from heaven saying unto them, Come up hither. And they ascended up to heaven in a cloud; and their enemies beheld them.

13. And the same hour was there a great earthquake, and the tenth part of the city fell, and in the earthquake were slain of men seven thousand: and the remnant were affrighted, and gave glory to the God of heaven.

14. The second woe is past; and, behold, the third woe cometh quickly.

15. And the seventh angel sounded; and there were great voices in heaven, saying, The kingdoms of this world are become the kingdoms of our Lord, and of his Christ; and he shall reign for ever and ever.

16. And the four and twenty elders, which sat before God on their seats, fell upon their faces, and worshipped God.

17. Saying, We give thee thanks, O Lord God Almighty, which art, and wast, and art to come; because thou hast taken to thee thy great power, and hast reigned.

18. And the nations were angry, and thy wrath is come, and the time of the dead, that they should be judged, and that thou shouldest give reward unto thy servants the prophets, and to the saints, and them that fear thy name, small and great; and shouldest destroy them which destroy the earth.

19. And the temple of God was opened in heaven, and there was seen in His temple the ark of His testament: and there were lightnings, and voices, and thunderings, and an earthquake, and great hail.

Revelation 12

1. And there appeared a great wonder in heaven; a woman clothed with the sun, and the moon under her feet, and upon her head a crown of twelve stars.

2. And she being with child cried, travailing in birth, and pained to be delivered.

3. And there appeared another wonder in heaven; and behold a great red dragon, having seven heads and ten horns, and seven crowns upon his heads.

4. And his tail drew the third part of the stars of heaven, and did cast them to the earth: and the dragon stood before the woman which was ready to be delivered, for to devour her child as soon as it was born.

5. And she brought forth a man child, who was to rule all nations with a rod of iron: and her child was caught up unto God, and to his throne.

6. And the woman fled into the wilderness, where she hath a place prepared of God, that they should feed her there a thousand two hundred and threescore days.

7. And there was war in heaven: Michael and his angels fought against the dragon; and the dragon fought and his angels.

8. And prevailed not; neither was their place found any more in heaven.

9. And the great dragon was cast out, that old serpent, called the Devil, and Satan, which deceiveth the whole world: he was cast out into the earth, and his angels were cast out with him.

10. And I heard a loud voice saying in heaven, Now is come salvation, and strength, and the kingdom of our God, and the power of his Christ: for the accuser of our brethren is cast down, which accused them before our God day and night.

11. And they overcame him by the blood of the Lamb, and by the word of their testimony; and they loved not their lives unto the death.

12. Therefore rejoice, ye heavens, and ye that dwell in them. Woe to the inhabiters of the earth and of the sea! for the devil is come down unto you, having great wrath, because he knoweth that he hath but a short time.

13. And when the dragon saw that he was cast unto the earth, he persecuted the woman which brought forth the man child.

14. And to the woman were given two wings of a great eagle, that she might fly into the wilderness, into her place, where she is nourished for a time, and times, and half a time, from the face of the serpent.
15. And the serpent cast out of his mouth water as a flood after the woman, that he might cause her to be carried away of the flood.
16. And the earth helped the woman, and the earth opened her mouth, and swallowed up the flood which the dragon cast out of his mouth.
17. And the dragon was wroth with the woman, and went to make war with the remnant of her seed, which keep the commandments of God, and have the testimony of Jesus Christ.

Revelation 13

1. And I stood upon the sand of the sea, and saw a beast rise up out of the sea, having seven heads and ten horns, and upon his horns ten crowns, and upon his heads the name of blasphemy.
2. And the beast which I saw was like unto a leopard, and his feet were as the feet of a bear, and his mouth as the mouth of a lion: and the dragon gave him his power, and his seat, and great authority.
3. And I saw one of his heads as it were wounded to death; and his deadly wound was healed: and all the world wondered after the beast.
4. And they worshipped the dragon which gave power unto the beast: and they worshipped the beast, saying, Who is like unto the beast? who is able to make war with him?
5. And there was given unto him a mouth speaking great things and blasphemies; and power was given unto him to continue forty and two months.
6. And he opened his mouth in blasphemy against God, to blaspheme his name, and his tabernacle, and them that dwell in heaven.

7. And it was given unto him to make war with the saints, and to overcome them: and power was given him over all kindreds, and tongues, and nations.
8. And all that dwell upon the earth shall worship him, whose names are not written in the book of life of the Lamb slain from the foundation of the world.
9. If any man have an ear, let him hear.
10. He that leadeth into captivity shall go into captivity: he that killeth with the sword must be killed with the sword. Here is the patience and the faith of the saints.
11. And I beheld another beast coming up out of the earth; and he had two horns like a lamb, and he spake as a dragon.
12. And he exerciseth all the power of the first beast before him, and causeth the earth and them which dwell therein to worship the first beast, whose deadly wound was healed.
13. And he doeth great wonders, so that he maketh fire come down from heaven on the earth in the sight of men.
14. And deceiveth them that dwell on the earth by the means of those miracles which he had power to do in the sight of the beast; saying to them that dwell on the earth, that they should make an image to the beast, which had the wound by a sword, and did live.
15. And he had power to give life unto the image of the beast, that the image of the beast should both speak, and cause that as many as would not worship the image of the beast should be killed.
16. And he causeth all, both small and great, rich and poor, free and bond, to receive a mark in their right hand, or in their foreheads.
17. And that no man might buy or sell, save he that had the mark, or the name of the beast, or the number of his name.
18. Here is wisdom. Let him that hath understanding count the number of the beast: for it is the number of a man; and his number is six hundred threescore and six.

Revelation 14

1. And I looked, and, lo, a Lamb stood on the mount Sion, and with him a hundred forty and four thousand, having his Father's name written in their foreheads.

2. And I heard a voice from heaven, as the voice of many waters, and as the voice of a great thunder: and I heard the voice of harpers harping with their harps.

3. And they sung as it were a new song before the throne, and before the four beasts, and the elders: and no man could learn that song but the hundred and forty and four thousand, which were redeemed from the earth.

4. These are they which were not defiled with women; for they are virgins. These are they which follow the Lamb whithersoever he goeth. These were redeemed from among men, being the first fruits unto God and to the Lamb.

5. And in their mouth was found no guile: for they are without fault before the throne of God.

6. And I saw another angel fly in the midst of heaven, having the everlasting gospel to preach unto them that dwell on the earth, and to every nation, and kindred, and tongue, and people.

7. Saying with a loud voice, Fear God, and give glory to Him; for the hour of His judgment is come: and worship Him that made heaven, and earth, and the sea, and the fountains of waters.

8. And there followed another angel, saying, Babylon is fallen, is fallen, that great city, because she made all nations drink of the wine of the wrath of her fornication.

9. And the third angel followed them, saying with a loud voice, If any man worship the beast and his image, and receive his mark in his forehead, or in his hand.

10. The same shall drink of the wine of the wrath of God, which is poured out without mixture into the cup of his indignation; and he shall be tormented with fire and brim-

stone in the presence of the holy angels, and in the presence of the Lamb.

11. And the smoke of their torment ascendeth up for ever and ever: and they have no rest day nor night, who worship the beast and his image, and whosoever receiveth the mark of his name.

12. Here is the patience of the saints: here are they that keep the commandments of God, and the faith of Jesus.

13. And I heard a voice from heaven saying unto me, Write, Blessed are the dead which die in the Lord from henceforth: Yea, saith the Spirit, that they may rest from their labours; and their works do follow them.

14. And I looked, and behold a white cloud, and upon the cloud one sat like unto the Son of man, having on His head a golden crown, and in His hand a sharp sickle.

15. And another angel came out of the temple, crying with a loud voice to him that sat on the cloud, Thrust in thy sickle, and reap: for the time is come for thee to reap; for the harvest of the earth is ripe.

16. And he that sat on the cloud thrust in his sickle on the earth; and the earth was reaped.

17. And another angel came out of the temple which is in heaven, he also having a sharp sickle.

18. And another angel came out from the altar, which had power over fire; and cried with a loud cry to him that had the sharp sickle, saying, Thrust in thy sharp sickle, and gather the clusters of the vine of the earth; for her grapes are fully ripe.

19. And the angel thrust in his sickle into the earth, and gathered the vine of the earth, and cast it into the great winepress of the wrath of God.

20. And the winepress was trodden without the city, and blood came out of the winepress, even unto the horse bridles, by the space of a thousand and six hundred furlongs.

Revelation 15

1. And I saw another sign in heaven, great and marvelous, seven angels having the seven last plagues; for in them is filled up the wrath of God.
2. And I saw as it were a sea of glass mingled with fire: and them that had gotten the victory over the beast, and over his image, and over his mark, and over the number of his name, stand on the sea of glass, having the harps of God.
3. And they sing the song of Moses the servant of God, and the song of the Lamb, saying, Great and marvelous are thy works, Lord God Almighty; just and true are thy ways, thou King of saints.
4. Who shall not fear thee, O Lord, and glorify thy name? for thou only art holy: for all nations shall come and worship before thee; for thy judgments are made manifest.
5. And after that I looked, and, behold, the temple of the tabernacle of the testimony in heaven was opened.
6. And the seven angels came out of the temple, having the seven plagues, clothed in pure and white linen, and having their breasts girded with golden girdles.
7. And one of the four beasts gave unto the seven angels seven golden vials full of the wrath of God, who liveth for ever and ever.
8. And the temple was filled with smoke from the glory of God, and from his power; and no man was able to enter into the temple, till the seven plagues of the seven angels were fulfilled.

Revelation 16

1. And I heard a great voice out of the temple saying to the seven angels, Go your ways, and pour out the vials of the wrath of God upon the earth.
2. And the first went, and poured out his vial upon the earth; and there fell a noisome and grievous sore upon the men

which had the mark of the beast, and upon them which worshipped his image.

3. And the second angel poured out his vial upon the sea; and it became as the blood of a dead man: and every living soul died in the sea.

4. And the third angel poured out his vial upon the rivers and fountains of waters; and they became blood.

5. And I heard the angel of the waters say, Thou art righteous, O Lord, which art, and wast, and shalt be, because thou hast judged thus.

6. For they have shed the blood of saints and prophets, and thou hast given them blood to drink; for they are worthy.

7. And I heard another out of the altar say, Even so, Lord God Almighty, true and righteous are thy judgments.

8. And the fourth angel poured out his vial upon the sun; and power was given unto him to scorch men with fire.

9. And men were scorched with great heat, and blasphemed the name of God, which hath power over these plagues: and they repented not to give him glory.

10. And the fifth angel poured out his vial upon the seat of the beast; and his kingdom was full of darkness; and they gnawed their tongues for pain.

11. And blasphemed the God of heaven because of their pains and their sores, and repented not of their deeds.

12. And the sixth angel poured out his vial upon the great river Euphrates; and the water thereof was dried up, that the way of the kings of the east might be prepared.

13. And I saw three unclean spirits like frogs come out of the mouth of the dragon, and out of the mouth of the beast, and out of the mouth of the false prophet.

14. For they are the spirits of devils, working miracles, which go forth unto the kings of the earth and of the whole world, to gather them to the battle of that great day of God Almighty.

15. Behold, I come as a thief. Blessed is he that watcheth, and keepeth his garments, lest he walk naked, and they see his shame.

16. And he gathered them together into a place called in the Hebrew tongue Armageddon.
17. And the seventh angel poured out his vial into the air; and there came a great voice out of the temple of heaven, from the throne, saying, It is done.
18. And there were voices, and thunders, and lightnings; and there was a great earthquake, such as was not since men were upon the earth, so mighty an earthquake, and so great.
19. And the great city was divided into three parts, and the cities of the nations fell: and great Babylon came in remembrance before God, to give unto her the cup of the wine of the fierceness of His wrath.
20. And every island fled away, and the mountains were not found.
21. And there fell upon men a great hail out of heaven, every stone about the weight of a talent: and men blasphemed God because of the plague of the hail; for the plague thereof was exceeding great.

Revelation 17

1. And there came one of the seven angels which had the seven vials, and talked with me, saying unto me, Come hither; I will shew unto thee the judgment of the great whore that sitteth upon many waters:
2. With whom the kings of the earth have committed fornication, and the inhabitants of the earth have been made drunk with the wine of her fornication.
3. So he carried me away in the spirit into the wilderness: and I saw a woman sit upon a scarlet coloured beast, full of names of blasphemy, having seven heads and ten horns.
4. And the woman was arrayed in purple and scarlet colour, and decked with gold and precious stones and pearls, having a golden cup in her hand full of abominations and filthiness of her fornication:

5. And upon her forehead was a name written, MYSTERY, BAB-
    YLON THE GREAT, THE MOTHER OF HARLOTS AND ABOMINA-
    TIONS OF THE EARTH.

6. And I saw the woman drunken with the blood of the saints,
    and with the blood of the martyrs of Jesus: and when I saw
    her, I wondered with great admiration.

7. And the angel said unto me, Wherefore didst thou marvel?
    I will tell thee the mystery of the woman, and of the beast
    that carrieth her, which hath the seven heads and ten horns.

8. The beast that thou sawest was, and is not; and shall ascend
    out of the bottomless pit, and go into perdition: and they
    that dwell on the earth shall wonder, whose names were
    not written in the book of life from the foundation of the
    world, when they behold the beast that was, and is not,
    and yet is.

9. And here is the mind which hath wisdom. The seven heads
    are seven mountains, on which the woman sitteth.

10. And there are seven kings: five are fallen, and one is, and
    the other is not yet come; and when he cometh, he must
    continue a short space.

11. And the beast that was, and is not, even he is the eighth,
    and is of the seven, and goeth into perdition.

12. And the ten horns which thou sawest are ten kings, which
    have received no kingdom as yet; but receive power as kings
    one hour with the beast.

13. These have one mind, and shall give their power and
    strength unto the beast.

14. These shall make war with the Lamb, and the Lamb shall
    overcome them: for he is Lord of lords, and King of kings: and
    they that are with him are called, and chosen, and faithful.

15. And he saith unto me, The waters which thou sawest,
    where the whore sitteth, are peoples, and multitudes, and
    nations, and tongues.

16. And the ten horns which thou sawest upon the beast,
    these shall hate the whore, and shall make her desolate and
    naked, and shall eat her flesh, and burn her with fire.

17. For God hath put in their hearts to fulfil His will, and to agree, and give their kingdom unto the beast, until the words of God shall be fulfilled.
18. And the woman which thou sawest is that great city, which reigneth over the kings of the earth.

Revelation 18

1. And after these things I saw another angel come down from heaven, having great power; and the earth was lightened with his glory.
2. And he cried mightily with a strong voice, saying, Babylon the great is fallen, is fallen, and is become the habitation of devils, and the hold of every foul spirit, and a cage of every unclean and hateful bird.
3. For all nations have drunk of the wine of the wrath of her formication, and the kings of the earth have committed fornication with her, and the merchants of the earth are waxed rich through the abundance of her delicacies. I
4. And I heard another voice from heaven, saying, Come out of her, my people, that ye be not partakers of her sins, and that ye receive not of her plagues.
5. For her sins have reached unto heaven, and God hath remembered her iniquities.
6. Reward her even as she rewarded you, and double unto her double according to her works: in the cup which she hath filled fill to her double.
7. How much she hath glorified herself, and lived deliciously, so much torment and sorrow give her: for she saith in her heart, I sit a queen, and am no widow, and shall see no sorrow.
8. Therefore shall her plagues come in one day, death, and mourning, and famine; and she shall be utterly burned with fire: for strong is the Lord God who judgeth her.
9. And the kings of the earth, who have committed formication and lived deliciously with her, shall bewail her,

and lament for her, when they shall see the smoke of her burning,

10. Standing afar off for the fear of her torment, saying, Alas, alas that great city Babylon, that mighty city! for in one hour is thy judgment come.

11. And the merchants of the earth shall weep and mourn over her; for no man buyeth their merchandise any more.

12. The merchandise of gold, and silver, and precious stones, and of pearls, and fine linen, and purple, and silk, and scarlet, and all thyine wood, and all manner vessels of ivory, and all manner vessels of most precious wood, and of brass, and iron, and marble.

13. And cinnamon, and odours, and ointments, and frankincense, and wine, and oil, and fine flour, and wheat, and beasts, and sheep, and horses, and chariots, and slaves, and souls of men.

14. And the fruits that thy soul lusted after are departed from thee, and all things which were dainty and goodly are departed from thee, and thou shalt find them no more at all.

15. The merchants of these things, which were made rich by her, shall stand afar off for the fear of her torment, weeping and wailing.

16. And saying, Alas, alas that great city, that was clothed in fine linen, and purple, and scarlet, and decked with gold, and precious stones, and pearls!

17. For in one hour so great riches is come to nought. And every shipmaster, and all the company in ships, and sailors, and as many as trade by sea, stood afar off,

18. And cried when they saw the smoke of her burning, saying, What city is like unto this great city!

19. And they cast dust on their heads, and cried, weeping and wailing, saying, Alas, alas that great city, wherein were made rich all that had ships in the sea by reason of her costliness for in one hour is she made desolate.

20. Rejoice over her, thou heaven, and ye holy apostles and prophets; for God hath avenged you on her.

21. And a mighty angel took up a stone like a great millstone, and cast it into the sea, saying, Thus with violence shall that great city Babylon be thrown down, and shall be found no more at all.

22. And the voice of harpers, and musicians, and of pipers, and trumpeters, shall be heard no more at all in thee; and no craftsman, of whatsoever craft he be, shall be found any more in thee; and the sound of a millstone shall be heard no more at all in thee.

23. And the light of a candle shall shine no more at all in thee; and the voice of the bridegroom and of the bride shall be heard no more at all in thee: for thy merchants were the great men of the earth; for by thy sorceries were all nations deceived.

24. And in her was found the blood of prophets, and of saints, and of all that were slain upon the earth.

Revelation 19

1. And after these things I heard a great voice of much people in heaven, saying, Alleluia; Salvation, and glory, and honour, and power, unto the Lord our God.

2. For true and righteous are his judgments: for he hath judged the great whore, which did corrupt the earth with her fornication, and hath avenged the blood of his servants at her hand.

3. And again they said, Alleluia And her smoke rose up for ever and ever.

4. And the four and twenty elders and the four beasts fell down and worshipped God that sat on the throne, saying, Amen; Alleluia.

5. And a voice came out of the throne, saying, Praise our God, all ye his servants, and ye that fear him, both small and great.

6. And I heard as it were the voice of a great multitude, and as the voice of many waters, and as the voice of mighty thunderings, saying, Alleluia: for the Lord God omnipotent reigneth.

7. Let us be glad and rejoice, and give honour to him: for the marriage of the Lamb is come, and his wife hath made herself ready.

8. And to her was granted that she should be arrayed in fine linen, clean and white: for the fine linen is the righteousness of saints.

9. And he saith unto me, Write, Blessed are they which are called unto the marriage supper of the Lamb. And he saith unto me, These are the true sayings of God.

10. And I fell at his feet to worship him. And he said unto me, See thou do it not: I am thy fellow servant, and of thy brethren that have the testimony of Jesus: worship God: for the testimony of Jesus is the spirit of prophecy.

11. And I saw heaven opened, and behold a white horse; and he that sat upon him was called Faithful and True, and in righteousness he doth judge and make war.

12. His eyes were as a flame of fire, and on his head were many crowns; and he had a name written, that no man knew, but he himself.

13. And he was clothed with a vesture dipped in blood: and his name is called The Word of God.

14. And the armies which were in heaven followed him upon white horses, clothed in fine linen, white and clean.

15. And out of his mouth goeth a sharp sword, that with it he should smite the nations: and he shall rule them with a rod of iron: and he treadeth the winepress of the fierceness and wrath of Almighty God.

16. And he hath on his vesture and on his thigh a name written, KING OF KINGS, AND LORD OF LORDS.

17. And I saw an angel standing in the sun; and he cried with a loud voice, saying to all the fowls that fly in the midst of heaven, Come and gather yourselves together unto the supper of the great God.

18. That ye may eat the flesh of kings, and the flesh of captains, and the flesh of mighty men, and the flesh of horses, and of

them that sit on them, and the flesh of all men, both free
and bond, both small and great.

19. And I saw the beast, and the kings of the earth, and their
armies, gathered together to make war against him that sat
on the horse, and against his army.

20. And the beast was taken, and with him the false prophet
that wrought miracles before him, with which he deceived
them that had received the mark of the beast, and them
that worshipped his image. These both were cast alive into
a lake of fire burning with brimstone.

21. And the remnant were slain with the sword of him that sat
upon the horse, which sword proceeded out of his mouth:
and all the fowls were filled with their flesh.

Revelation 20

1. And I saw an angel come down from heaven, having the
key of the bottomless pit and a great chain in his hand.

2. And he laid hold on the dragon, that old serpent, which
is the Devil, and Satan, and bound him a thousand years.

3. And cast him into the bottomless pit, and shut him up, and
set a seal upon him, that he should deceive the nations no
more, till the thousand years should be fulfilled: and after
that he must be loosed a little season.

4. And I saw thrones, and they sat upon them, and judgment
was given unto them: and I saw the souls of them that
were beheaded for the witness of Jesus, and for the word of
God, and which had not worshipped the beast, neither his
image, neither had received his mark upon their foreheads,
or in their hands; and they lived and reigned with Christ a
thousand years.

5. But the rest of the dead lived not again until the thousand
years were finished. This is the first resurrection.

6. Blessed and holy is he that hath part in the first resurrection: on such the second death hath no power, but they

shall be priests of God and of Christ, and shall reign with him a thousand years.

7. And when the thousand years are expired, Satan shall be loosed out of his prison.

8. And shall go out to deceive the nations which are in the four quarters of the earth, Gog, and Magog, to gather them together to battle: the number of whom is as the sand of the sea.

9. And they went up on the breadth of the earth, and compassed the camp of the saints about, and the beloved city: and fire came down from God out of heaven, and devoured them.

10. And the devil that deceived them was cast into the lake of fire and brimstone, where the beast and the false prophet are, and shall be tormented day and night for ever and ever.

11. And I saw a great white throne, and him that sat on it, from whose face the earth and the heaven fled away; and there was found no place for them.

12. And I saw the dead, small and great, stand before God; and the books were opened: and another book was opened, which is the book of life: and the dead were judged out of those things which were written in the books, according to their works.

13. And the sea gave up the dead which were in it; and death and hell delivered up the dead which were in them: and they were judged every man according to their works.

14. And death and hell were cast into the lake of fire. This is the second death.

15. And whosoever was not found written in the book of life was cast into the lake of fire.

Revelation 21

1. And I saw a new heaven and a new earth: for the first heaven and the first earth were passed away; and there was no more sea.

2. And I John saw the holy city, new Jerusalem, coming down from God out of heaven, prepared as a bride adorned for her husband.

3. And I heard a great voice out of heaven saying, Behold, the tabernacle of God is with men, and he will dwell with them, and they shall be his people, and God himself shall be with them, and be their God.

4. And God shall wipe away all tears from their eyes; and there shall be no more death, neither sorrow, nor crying, neither shall there be any more pain: for the former things are passed away.

5. And he that sat upon the throne said, Behold, I make all things new. And he said unto me, Write: for these words are true and faithful.

6. And he said unto me, It is done. I am Alpha and Omega, the beginning and the end. I will give unto him that is athirst of the fountain of the water of life freely.

7. He that overcometh shall inherit all things; and I will be his God, and he shall be my son.

8. But the fearful, and unbelieving, and the abominable, and murderers, and whoremongers, and sorcerers, and idolaters, and all liars, shall have their part in the lake which burneth with fire and brimstone: which is the second death.

9. And there came unto me one of the seven angels which had the seven vials full of the seven last plagues, and talked with me, saying, Come hither, I will shew thee the bride, the Lamb's wife.

10. And he carried me away in the spirit to a great and high mountain, and shewed me that great city, the holy Jerusalem, descending out of heaven from God,

11. Having the glory of God: and her light was like unto a stone most precious, even like a jasper stone, clear as crystal;

12. And had a wall great and high, and had twelve gates, and at the gates twelve angels, and names written thereon, which are the names of the twelve tribes of the children of Israel:

13. On the east three gates; on the north three gates; on the south three gates; and on the west three gates.
14. And the wall of the city had twelve foundations, and in them the names of the twelve apostles of the Lamb.
15. And he that talked with me had a golden reed to measure the city, and the gates thereof, and the wall thereof.
16. And the city lieth foursquare, and the length is as large as the breadth: and he measured the city with the reed, twelve thousand furlongs. The length and the breadth and the height of it are equal.
17. And he measured the wall thereof, a hundred and forty and four cubits, according to the measure of a man, that is, of the angel.
18. And the building of the wall of it was of jasper: and the city was pure gold, like unto clear glass.
19. And the foundations of the wall of the city were garnished with all manner of precious stones. The first foundation was jasper; the second, sapphire; the third, a chalcedony; the fourth, an emerald.
20. The fifth, sardonyx; the sixth, sardius; the seventh, chrysolyte; the eighth, beryl; the ninth, a topaz; the tenth, a chrysoprasus; the eleventh, a jacinth; the twelfth, an amethyst.
21. And the twelve gates were twelve pearls: every several gate was of one pearl: and the street of the city was pure gold, as it were transparent glass.
22. And I saw no temple therein: for the Lord God Almighty and the Lamb are the temple of it.
23. And the city had no need of the sun, neither of the moon, to shine in it: for the glory of God did lighten it, and the Lamb is the light thereof.
24. And the nations of them which are saved shall walk in the light of it: and the kings of the earth do bring their glory and honour into it.
25. And the gates of it shall not be shut at all by day: for there shall be no night there.

26. And they shall bring the glory and honour of the nations into it.
27. And there shall in no wise enter into it anything that defileth, neither whatsoever worketh abomination, or maketh a lie: but they which are written in the Lamb's book of life.

Revelation 22

1. And he shewed me a pure river of water of life, clear as crystal, proceeding out of the throne of God and of the Lamb.
2. In the midst of the street of it, and on either side of the river, was there the tree of life, which bare twelve manner of fruits, and yielded her fruit every month: and the leaves of the tree were for the healing of the nations.
3. And there shall be no more curse: but the throne of God and of the Lamb shall be in it; and his servants shall serve him.
4. And they shall see his face; and his name shall be in their foreheads.
5. And there shall be no night there; and they need no candle, neither light of the sun; for the Lord God giveth them light: and they shall reign for ever and ever.
6. And he said unto me, These sayings are faithful and true: and the Lord God of the holy prophets sent his angel to shew unto his servants the things which must shortly be done.
7. Behold, I come quickly: blessed is he that keepeth the sayings of the prophecy of this book.
8. And I John saw these things, and heard them. And when I had heard and seen, I fell down to worship before the feet of the angel which shewed me these things.
9. Then saith he unto me, See thou do it not: for I am thy fellow servant, and of thy brethren the prophets, and of them which keep the sayings of this book: worship God.

10. And he saith unto me, Seal not the sayings of the prophecy of this book: for the time is at hand.

11. He that is unjust, let him be unjust still: and he which is filthy, let him be filthy still: and he that is righteous, let him be righteous still: and he that is holy, let him be holy still.

12. And, behold, I come quickly; and my reward is with me, to give every man according as his work shall be.

13. I am Alpha and Omega, the beginning and the end, the first and the last.

14. Blessed are they that do his commandments, that they may have right to the tree of life, and may enter in through the gates into the city.

15. For without are dogs, and sorcerers, and whoremongers, and murderers, and idolaters, and whosoever loveth and maketh a lie.

16. I Jesus have sent mine angel to testify unto you these things in the churches. I am the root and the offspring of David, and the bright and morning star.

17. And the Spirit and the bride say, Come. And let him that heareth say, Come. And let him that is athirst come. And whosoever will, let him take the water of life freely.

18. For I testify unto every man that heareth the words of the prophecy of this book, If any man shall add unto these things, God shall add unto him the plagues that are written in this book:

19. And if any man shall take away from the words of the book of this prophecy, God shall take away his part out of the book of life, and out of the holy city, and from the things which are written in this book.

20. He which testifieth these things saith, Surely I come quickly. Amen. Even so, come, Lord Jesus.

21. The grace of our Lord Jesus Christ be with you all. Amen.

Faith Is
A poem by Sis. Halima

Faith is the way that we all can come in
They say it's the only sure way
Faith is what took away all of my sins
They say that Christ died one day
Faith is what brought me from death to life be
Cause I have faith in Christ's sacrifice
Faith is the door so we all can come in
We'll rejoice with the Lord and win
Faith is what conquered the devils below
They've been conquered for you and for me
Faith lets us see their deception, you know
Through faith we have victory
Faith is the key that will open the door
It will let us know
What the Lord has us here for
Faith gives us strength to endure to the end
We'll rejoice with the Lord and win
Faith is what separates the bound from the free
You're in bondage when you don't believe
Faith will escort us to eternity
It's our faith that will make us achieve
Faith is what gives us the privilege to be
The called, the adopted, the royal family
Faith is the gift that the lord gives us free
We'll rejoice with the Lord and win

*Now faith is the substance of things hoped
for, the evidence of things not seen.*
—Hebrews 11:1

And I appointed the eighth day also, that the eighth day should be the first-created after my work, and that the first seven revolve in the form of the seventh thousand, and that at the beginning of the eighth thousand there should be a time of not-counting, endless, with neither years nor months nor weeks nor days nor hours *(Enoch XXXIII)*.

6

The Eighth Day

And God shall wipe away all tears from their
eyes; and there shall be no more death,
neither sorrow, nor crying, neither shall there be any more pain:
for the former things are passed away.
—Revelation 21:4

God Is!
A poem by Sis. Halima

God is perfect
God is just
God knows every single one of us
God is loving
He knows what is true
He sent His only son down
To die for me and you
God is righteous
He makes it plain to see
That whosoever believe in Christ
Will have eternity
God is holy
He sets us all apart
He lets us know each one is judged
By what is in His heart
God is eternal
He's been here from the start
He made the sun, the moon, the stars
And spaced each one apart
God is our Father
For those who believe in Christ
He lets us all rejoice with him
Because of Christ's sacrifice.

God is a spirit: and they that worship him
must worship him in spirit and in truth.
—John 4:24

The Eighth Day

And I appointed the eighth day also, that the eighth day should be the first-created after my work, and that the first seven revolve in the form of the seventh thousand, and that at the beginning of the eighth thousand there should be a time of not-counting, endless, with neither years nor months nor weeks nor days nor hours (Enoch XXXIII).

To him that overcometh will I give to eat of the tree of life, which is in the midst of the paradise of God (Rev. 2:7).

He that overcometh shall not be hurt of the second death (Rev. 2:11).

To him that overcometh will I give to eat of the hidden manna, and will give him a white stone, and in the stone a new name written, which no man knoweth saving he that receiveth it (Rev. 2:17).

And he that overcometh, and keepeth my works unto the end, to him will I give power over the nations (Rev. 2:26).

And he shall rule them with a rod of iron; as the vessels of a potter shall they be broken to shivers: even as I received of my Father (Rev. 2:27).

And I will give him the morning star (Rev. 2:28).

He that overcometh, the same shall be clothed in white raiment; and I will not blot out his name out of the book of life, but I will confess his name before my Father, and before his angels (Rev. 3:5).

Behold, I will make them of the synagogue of Satan, which say they are Jews, and are not, but do lie; behold, I will make them to come and worship before thy feet, and to know that I have loved thee (Rev. 3:9).

Because thou hast kept the word of my patience, I also will keep thee from the hour of temptation, which shall come upon all the world, to try them that dwell upon the earth (Rev. 3:10).

Him that overcometh will I make a pillar in the temple of my God, and he shall go no more out: and I will write upon him the name of my God, and the name of the city of my God, which is new Jerusalem, which cometh down out of heaven from my God: and I will write upon him my new name (Rev. 3:12).

To him that overcometh will I grant to sit with me in my throne, even as I also overcame, and am set down with my Father in his throne (Rev. 3:21).

And I saw a new heaven and a new earth: for the first heaven and the first earth were passed away; and there was no more sea.

And I John saw the holy city, new Jerusalem, coming down from God out of heaven, prepared as a bride adorned for her husband.

And I heard a great voice out of heaven saying, Behold, the tabernacle of God is with men, and he will dwell with them, and they shall be his people, and God himself shall be with them, and be their God.

And God shall wipe away all tears from their eyes; and there shall be no more death, neither sorrow, nor crying, neither shall there be any more pain: for the former things are passed away (Rev. 21:1, 4).

5. When all creation visible and invisible, as the Lord created it, shall end, then every man goes to the great judgement, and then all time shall perish, and the years, and thenceforward there will be neither months nor days nor hours, they will be stuck together and will not be counted.

6. There will be one aeon, and all the righteous who shall escape the Lord's great judgement, shall be collected in the great aeon, for the righteous the great aeon will begin, and they will live eternally, and then too there will be amongst them neither labour, nor sickness, nor humiliation, nor anxiety, nor need, nor violence, nor night, nor darkness, but great light.

7. And they shall have a great indestructible wall, and a paradise bright and incorruptible, for all corruptible things shall pass away, and there will be eternal life (Enoch LXV:5–7).

Enoch LXVI:7

7. Walk, my children, in longsuffering, in meekness, honesty, in provocation, in grief, in faith and in truth, in reliance on promises, in illness, in abuse, in wounds, in temptation, in nakedness, in privation, loving one another, till you go out from this age of ills, that you become inheritors of endless time.

We're Never Alone!
A poem by Sis. Halima

When special people touch our lives
Then suddenly we see
How beautiful and wonderful
The world can really be
It's good to know within our hearts
That there's someone who cares
It's good to know we're not alone
There's someone standing there
I know of someone in my life
Who cares so much for me
He took upon my sins
And he died on Calvary
I will never leave you nor forsake you
That's the words he said to me
As I read his words continuously
I can see his victory
And now I know I'm not alone
I'm not all by myself
I see the world through his eyes
That joy is much better than wealth
I see the world is not my home
It is just aplace to be
He's gone to prepare a place for me
And my brand-new family

Let your conversation be without covetousness;
and be content with such things as ye have
for he hath said, I will never leave
thee, nor forsake thee.
—Hebrews 13:5

For I have learned to be content in whatever circumstances I am. I know how to get along with humble means, and I also know how to live in prosperity; in any and every circumstance I have learned the secret of being filled and going hungry, both of having abundance and suffering need. I can do all things through Him who strengthens me. *(Phil. 4:11b–13)*

7

Forty Things God Provides Every Believer at the Moment of Salvation

Have Faith in the Lord!

A poem by Sis. Halima

When things come down all around you
You have to have faith in the Lord.
When nothing but trouble surrounds you
You have to have faith in the Lord.
Don't look down in shame
just call on his name.
He'll give you the strength to endure.
When people speak false things about you
you have to have faith in the Lord.
When the ones that you love, they shout too
you have to have faith in the Lord.
He'll speak of your name and
He will proclaim
eternity is your reward.
When drugs in our land upsets you
you have to have faith in the Lord.
And you say your family rejects you
Hey, you have to have faith in the Lord!
The Lord gives us hope to overcome dope
He protects us—our souls and our life.
In time we will see, our Families unity.
It was Christ that made the sacrifice

*But without faith it is impossible to please
him: For he that cometh to God must believe
That he is, and that he is a rewarder
of them That diligently seek him.*
—Hebrews 11:6

The Benefits of Salvation

1. The believer resides in the eternal plan of God (shares the destiny of Christ). He is:

   A. Foreknown:

   Him, being delivered by the determinate counsel and foreknowledge of God, ye have taken, and by wicked hands have crucified and slain. (Acts 2:23)

   For whom he did foreknow, he also did predestinate to be conformed to the image of his Son, that he might be the firstborn among many brethren. (Rom. 8:29).

   Elect according to the foreknowledge of God the Father, through sanctification of the Spirit, unto obedience and sprinkling of the blood of Jesus Christ: Grace unto you, and peace, be multiplied. (1 Pet. 1:2)

   B. Elected:

   Who shall lay anything to the charge of God's elect? It is God that justifieth. (Rom. 8:33)

   Put on therefore, as the elect of God, holy and beloved, bowels of mercies, kindness, humbleness of mind, meekness, longsuffering. (Col. 3:12)

   Knowing, brethren beloved, your election of God. (1 Thess. 1:4)

   Paul, a servant of God, and an apostle of Jesus Christ, according to the faith of God's elect, and the acknowledging of the truth which is after godliness. (Titus 1:1)

Elect according to the foreknowledge of God the Father, through sanctification of the Spirit, unto obedience and sprinkling of the blood of Jesus Christ: Grace unto you, and peace, be multiplied. (1 Pet. 1:2)

C. Predestined:

For whom he did foreknow, he also did predestinate to be conformed to the image of his Son, that he might be the firstborn among many brethren. Moreover whom he did predestinate, them he also called: and whom he called, them he also justified: and whom he justified, them he also glorified. (Rom. 8:29–30)

Having predestinated us unto the adoption of children by Jesus Christ to himself, according to the good pleasure of his will... In whom also we have obtained an inheritance, being predestinated according to the purpose of him who worketh all things after the counsel of his own will. (Eph. 1:5, 11)

D. Chosen:

For many are called, but few are chosen. (Matt. 22:14)

To whom coming, as unto a living stone, disallowed indeed of men, but chosen of God, and precious. (1 Pet. 2:4)

E. Called:

Faithful is he that calleth you, who also will do it. (1 Thess. 5:24)

2. The believer is reconciled (removal of the barrier between man and God)

A. By God:

And all things are of God, who hath reconciled us to himself by Jesus Christ, and hath given to us the ministry of reconciliation; To wit, that God was in Christ, reconciling the world unto himself, not imputing their trespasses unto them; and hath committed unto us the word of reconciliation. (2 Cor. 5:18–19)

And, having made peace through the blood of his cross, by him to reconcile all things unto himself; by him, I say, whether they be things in earth, or things in heaven. (Col. 1:20)

B. To God:

For if, when we were enemies, we were reconciled to God by the death of his Son, much more, being reconciled, we shall be saved by his life. (Rom. 5:10)

Now then we are ambassadors for Christ, as though God did beseech you by us: we pray you in Christ's stead, be ye reconciled to God. (2 Cor. 5:20)

For he is our peace, who hath made both one, and hath broken down the middle wall of partition between us; Having abolished in his flesh the enmity, even the law of commandments contained in ordinances; for to make in himself of twain one new man, so making peace; And that he might reconcile both unto God in one body by the cross, having slain the enmity thereby: And came and preached peace to you which were afar off, and to them that were nigh. (Eph. 2:14–17)

3. The believer is redeemed (purchased from the slave market of sin)

    Being justified freely by his grace through the redemption that is in Christ Jesus. (Rom. 3:24)

    In whom we have redemption through his blood, even the forgiveness of sins. (Col. 1:14)

    Forasmuch as ye know that ye were not redeemed with corruptible things, as silver and gold, from your vain conversation received by tradition from your fathers. (1 Pet. 1:18)

4. The believer's condemnation (eternal judgment) is removed:

    He that believeth on him is not condemned: but he that believeth not is condemned already, because he hath not believed in the name of the only begotten Son of God. (John 3:18)

    Verily, verily, I say unto you, He that heareth my word, and believeth on him that sent me, hath everlasting life, and shall not come into condemnation; but is passed from death unto life. (John 5:24)

There is therefore now no condemnation to them which are in Christ Jesus, who walk not after the flesh, but after the Spirit. (Rom. 8:1)

5. All sins are judged by the substitutionary spiritual death of Christ on the cross:

    Who was delivered for our offences, and was raised again for our justification. (Rom. 4:25)

    In whom we have redemption through his blood, the forgiveness of sins, according to the riches of his grace. (Eph. 1:7)

    Who his own self bare our sins in his own body on the tree, that we, being dead to sins, should live unto righteousness: by whose stripes ye were healed. (1 Pet. 2:24)

6. Every believer receives propitiation for sins (God satisfied with the work of His Son):

    Whom God hath set forth to be a propitiation through faith in his blood, to declare his righteousness for the remission of sins that are past, through the forbearance of God; To declare, I say, at this time his righteousness: that he might be just, and the justifier of him which believeth in Jesus. (Rom. 3:25–26)

    And he is the propitiation for our sins: and not for ours only, but also for the sins of the whole world. (1 John 2:2)

Herein is love, not that we loved God, but that he loved us, and sent his Son to be the propitiation for our sins. (1 John 4:10)

7. The believer is dead to old life (old sin nature), but alive to God (retroactive positional truth). He is:

A. Crucified with Christ:

Knowing this, that our old man is crucified with him, that the body of sin might be destroyed, that henceforth we should not serve sin. (Rom. 6:6)

I am crucified with Christ: nevertheless I live; yet not l, but Christ liveth in me: and the life which I now live in the flesh I live by the faith of the Son of God, who loved me, and gave himself for me. (Gal. 2:20)

B. Dead with Christ:

Now if we be dead with Christ, we believe that we shall also live with him. (Rom. 6:8)

For ye are dead, and your life is hid with Christ in God. (Col. 3:3)

Who his own self bare our sins in his own body on the tree, that we, being dead to sins, should live unto righteousness: by whose stripes ye were healed. (1 Pet. 2:24)

C. Buried with Christ:

Therefore we are buried with him by baptism into death: that like as Christ was raised up from the dead by the glory of the Father, even so we also should walk in newness of life. (Rom. 6:4)

Buried with him in baptism, wherein also ye are risen with him through the faith of the operation of God, who hath raised him from the dead. (Col. 2:12)

D. Raised with Christ:

Therefore we are buried with him by baptism into death: that like as Christ was raised up from the dead by the glory of the Father, even so we also should walk in newness of life. (Rom. 6:4)

If ye then be risen with Christ, seek those things which are above, where Christ sitteth on the right hand of God… But now ye also put off all these; anger, wrath, malice, blasphemy, filthy communication out of your mouth. (Col. 3:1, 8)

8. The believer is free from the Mosaic Law. He is:

A. Dead:

Wherefore, my brethren, ye also are become dead to the law by the body of Christ; that ye should be married to another, even to him who is raised from the dead, that we should bring forth fruit unto God. (Rom. 7:4)

B. Delivered:

For sin shall not have dominion over you: for ye are not under the law, but under grace. (Rom. 6:14)

But now we are delivered from the law, that being dead wherein we were held; that we should serve in newness of spirit, and not in the oldness of the letter. (Rom. 7:6)

For if that which is done away was glorious, much more that which remaineth is glorious. (2 Cor. 3:11)

But after that faith is come, we are no longer under a schoolmaster. (Gal. 3:25)

9. The believer is regenerated:

Jesus saith to him, He that is washed needeth not save to wash his feet, but is clean every whit: and ye are clean, but not all. (John 13:10)

And such were some of you: but ye are washed, but ye are sanctified, but ye are justified in the name of the Lord Jesus, and by the Spirit of our God. (1 Cor: 6:11)

Not by works of righteousness which we have done, but according to his mercy he saved us, by the washing of regeneration, and renewing of the Holy Ghost; (He is). (Titus 3:5)

A. Born again:

Marvel not that I said unto thee, Ye must be born again. (John 3:7)

Being born again, not of corruptible seed, but of incorruptible, by the word of God, which liveth and abideth forever. (1 Pet. 1:23)

B. A child of God:

>   For ye are all the children of God by faith in Christ Jesus. (Gal. 3:26)

C. A son of God:

>   But as many as received him, to them gave he power to become the sons of God, even to them that believe on his name. (John 1:12)

>   And will be a Father unto you, and ye shall be my sons and daughters, saith the Lord Almighty. (2 Cor. 6:18)

>   Beloved, now are we the sons of God, and it doth not yet appear what we shall be: but we know that, when he shall appear, we shall be like him; for we shall see him as he is. (1 John 3:2)

D. A new creation:

>   Therefore if any man be in Christ, he is a new creature: old things are passed away; behold, all things are become new. (2 Cor: 5:17)

>   For in Christ Jesus neither circumcision availeth anything, nor uncircumcision, but a new creature. (Gal. 6:15)

>   For we are his workmanship, created in Christ Jesus unto good works, which God hath before ordained that we should walk in them. (Eph. 2:10)

10. The believer is adopted by God (placed as adult sons because of positional truth):

> For ye have not received the spirit of bondage again to fear; but ye have received the Spirit of adoption, whereby we cry, Abba, Father. (Rom. 8:15)

> And not only they, but ourselves also, which have the first fruits of the Spirit, even we ourselves groan within ourselves, waiting for the adoption, to wit, the redemption of our body. (Rom. 8:23 [future])

> Having predestinated us unto the adoption of children by Jesus Christ to himself, according to the good pleasure of his will. (Eph. 1:5)

11. The believer is made acceptable to God:

> To the praise of the glory of his grace, wherein he hath made us accepted in the beloved. (Eph. 1:6)

> Ye also, as lively stones, are built up a spiritual house, a holy priesthood, to offer up spiritual sacrifices, acceptable to God by Jesus Christ (He is). (1 Pet. 2:5)

   A. Made righteous (imputation):

> Even the righteousness of God which is by faith of Jesus Christ unto all and upon all them that believe: for there is no difference. (Rom. 3:22)

> But of him are ye in Christ Jesus, who of God is made unto us wisdom, and righteousness, and sanctification, and redemption. (1 Con 1:30)

For he hath made him to be sin for us, who knew no sin; that we might be made the righteousness of God in him. (2 Cor. 5:21)

And be found in him, not having mine own righteousness, which is of the law, but that which is through the faith of Christ, the righteousness which is of God by faith. (Phil. 3:9)

B. Sanctified positionally

But of him are ye in Christ Jesus, who of God is made unto us wisdom, and righteousness, and sanctification, and redemption. (1 Cor. 1:30)

And such were some of you: but ye are washed, but ye are sanctified, but ye are justified in the name of the Lord Jesus, and by the Spirit of our God. (1 Cor. 6:11)

C. Perfected forever:

For by one offering he hath perfected forever them that are sanctified. (Heb. 10:14)

D. Qualified for inheritance:

Giving thanks unto the Father, which hath made us meet to be partakers of the inheritance of the saints in light. (Col. 1:12)

12. The believer is justified (declared righteous):

Being justified freely by his grace through the redemption that is in Christ Jesus. (Rom. 3:24)

Therefore being justified by faith, we have peace with God through our Lord Jesus Christ... Much more then, being now justified by his blood, we shall be saved from wrath through him. (Rom. 5:1, 9)

Moreover whom he did predestinate, them he also called: and whom he called, them he also justified: and whom he justified, them he also glorified. (Rom. 8:30)

And such were some of you: but ye are washed, but ye are sanctified, but ye are justified in the name of the Lord Jesus, and by the Spirit of our God. (1 Cor. 6:11)

That being justified by his grace, we should be made heirs according to the hope of eternal life. (Titus 3:7)

13. The believer receives the unique availability of divine power:

According as his divine power hath given unto us all things that pertain unto life and godliness, through the knowledge of him that hath called us to glory and virtue. (2 Pet. 1:3)

14. The believer is guaranteed a heavenly citizenship based on reconciliation:

Notwithstanding in this rejoice not, that the spirits are subject unto you; but rather rejoice, because your names are written in heaven. (Luke 10:20)

But now in Christ Jesus ye who sometimes were far off are made nigh by the blood of Christ...

Now therefore ye are no more strangers and foreigners, but fellow citizens with the saints, and of the household of God. (Eph. 2:13, 19)

For our conversation is in heaven; from whence also we look for the Saviour, the Lord Jesus Christ. (Phil. 3:20)

15. The believer is delivered from the kingdom of Satan:

Who hath delivered us from the power of darkness. (Col. 1:13a)

And having spoiled principalities and powers, he made a shew of them openly, triumphing over them in it. (Col. 2:15)

16. The believer is transferred into God's kingdom:

And hath translated us into the kingdom of his dear Son. (Col. 1:13b)

17. The believer is now on a secure foundation:

For other foundation can no man lay than that is laid, which is Jesus Christ. (1 Cor. 3:11)

And did all drink the same spiritual drink: for they drank of that spiritual Rock that followed them: and that Rock was Christ. (1 Cor. 10:4)

And are built upon the foundation of the apostles and prophets, Jesus Christ himself being the chief corner stone. (Eph. 2:20)

18. Every believer is a gift from God the Father to Christ:

> My Father, which gave them me, is greater than all; and no man is able to pluck them out of my Father's hand. (John 10:29)

> As thou hast given him power over all flesh, that he should give eternal life to as many as thou hast given him... I have manifested thy name unto the men which thou gavest me out of the world: thine they were, and thou gavest them me; and they have kept thy word... I pray for them: I pray not for the world, but for them which thou hast given me; for they are thine... And now I am no more in the world, but these are in the world, and I come to thee. Holy Father, keep through thine own name those whom thou hast given me, that they may be one, as we are. While I was with them in the world, I kept them in thy name: those that thou gavest me I have kept, and none of them is lost, but the son of perdition; that the scripture might be fulfilled... Father, I will that they also, whom thou hast given me, be with me where I am; that they may behold my glory, which thou hast given me: for thou lovedst me before the foundation of the world. (John 17:2, 6, 9, 11–12, 24)

19. The believer is delivered from the power of the sin nature:

> But he is a Jew, which is one inwardly; and circumcision is that of the heart, in the spirit, and not in the letter; whose praise is not of men, but of God. (Rom. 2:29)

> For we are the circumcision, which worship God in the spirit, and rejoice in Christ Jesus, and have no confidence in the flesh. (Phil. 3:3)

> In whom also ye are circumcised with the circumcision made without hands, in putting off the body of the sins of the flesh by the circumcision of Christ. (Col. 2:11)

20. Every believer is appointed a priest unto God. We are:

  A. A holy priesthood:

  > Ye also, as lively stones, are built up a spiritual house, a holy priesthood, to offer up spiritual sacrifices, acceptable to God by Jesus Christ. (1 Pet. 2:5)

  B. A royal priesthood:

  > But ye are a chosen generation, a royal priesthood, an holy nation, a peculiar people; that ye should shew forth the praises of him who hath called you out of darkness into his marvelous light. (1 Pet. 2:9)

  > And hath made us kings and priests unto God and his Father; to him be glory and dominion for ever and ever. Amen. (Rev. 1:6)

21. The believer receives eternal security:

  > He that spared not his own Son, but delivered him up for us all, how shall he not with him also freely give us all things? …For I am persuaded, that neither death, nor life, nor angels, nor principalities, nor powers, nor things present,

nor things to come, Nor height, nor depth, nor any other creature, shall be able to separate us from the love of God, which is in Christ Jesus our Lord. (Rom. 8:32, 38–39)

For ye are all the children of God by faith in Christ Jesus. (Gal. 3:26)

If we believe not, yet he abideth faithful: he cannot deny himself. (2 Tim. 2:13)

22. The believer is given access to God:

By whom also we have access by faith into this grace wherein we stand, and rejoice in hope of the glory of God. (Rom. 5:2)

For through him we both have access by one Spirit unto the Father. (Eph. 2:18)

Seeing then that we have a great high priest, that is passed into the heavens, Jesus the Son of God, let us hold fast our profession… Let us therefore come boldly unto the throne of grace, that we may obtain mercy, and find grace to help in time of need. (Heb. 4:14, 16)

Having therefore, brethren, boldness to enter into the holiest by the blood of Jesus, By a new and living way, which he hath consecrated for us, through the veil, that is to say, his flesh. (Heb. 10:19–20)

23. Every believer is within the "much more" grace care of God:

> Much more then, being now justified by his blood, we shall be saved from wrath through him. For if, when we were enemies, we were reconciled to God by the death of his Son, much more, being reconciled, we shall be saved by his life. (Rom. 5:9–10)

(We are):

A. Objects of His love:

> But God, who is rich in mercy, for his great love wherewith he loved us. (Eph. 2:4)

> And walk in love, as Christ also hath loved us, and hath given himself for us an offering and a sacrifice to God for a sweet smelling savour. (Eph. 5:2)

B. Objects of His grace

   (1) For salvation:

> For by grace are ye saved through faith; and that not of yourselves: it is the gift of God: Not of works, lest any man should boast. (Eph. 2:8–9)

   (2) For keeping:

> By whom also we have access by faith into this grace wherein we stand, and rejoice in hope of the glory of God. (Rom. 5:2)

Who are kept by the power of God through faith unto salvation ready to be revealed in the last time. (1 Pet. 1:5)

(3) For service:

As thou hast sent me into the world, even so have I also sent them into the world. (John 17:18)

But unto every one of us is given grace according to the measure of the gift of Christ. (Eph. 4:7)

(4) For instruction:

Teaching us that, denying ungodliness and worldly lusts, we should live soberly, righteously, and godly, in this present world. (Titus 2:12)

C. Objects of His power:

And what is the exceeding greatness of his power to us-ward who believe, according to the working of his mighty power. (Eph. 1:19)

For it is God which worketh in you both to will and to do of his good pleasure. (Phil. 2:13)

D. Objects of His faithfulness:

Being confident of this very thing, that he which hath begun a good work in you will perform it until the day of Jesus Christ. (Phil. 1:6)

For he hath said, I will never leave thee, nor forsake thee. (Heb. 13:5b)

E. Objects of His peace:

Peace I leave with you, my peace I give unto you: not as the world giveth, give I unto you. Let not your heart be troubled, neither let it be afraid. (John 14:27)

F. Objects of His consolation:

Now our Lord Jesus Christ himself, and God, even our Father, which hath loved us, and hath given us everlasting consolation and good hope through grace. (2 Thess. 2:16)

G. Objects of His intercession:

Who is he that condemneth? It is Christ that died, yea rather, that is risen again, who is even at the right hand of God, who also maketh intercession for us. (Rom. 8:34)

Wherefore he is able also to save them to the uttermost that come unto God by him, seeing he ever liveth to make intercession for them. (Heb. 7:25)

For Christ is not entered into the holy places made with hands, which are the figures of the true; but into heaven itself, now to appear in the presence of God for us. (Heb. 9:24)

24. The believer is beneficiary of an inheritance as heirs of God and joint-heirs with Christ:

> And if children, then heirs; heirs of God, and joint-heirs with Christ; if so be that we suffer with him, that we may be also glorified together. (Rom. 8:17)

> Which is the earnest of our inheritance until the redemption of the purchased possession, unto the praise of his glory... The eyes of your understanding being enlightened; that ye may know what is the hope of his calling, and what the riches of the glory of his inheritance in the saints. (Eph. 1:14, 18)

> Knowing that of the Lord ye shall receive the reward of the inheritance: for ye serve the Lord Christ. (Col. 3:24)

> And for this cause he is the mediator of the new testament, that by means of death, for the redemption of the transgressions that were under the first testament, they which are called might receive the promise of eternal inheritance. (Heb. 9:15)

> To an inheritance incorruptible, and undefiled, and that fadeth not away, reserved in heaven for you. (1 Pet. 1:4)

25. Every believer has a new position in Christ:

> And hath raised us up together, and made us sit together in heavenly places in Christ Jesus. (Eph. 2:6)

(We are):

A. Partners with Christ in life:

When Christ, who is our life, shall appear, then shall ye also appear with him in glory. (Col. 3:4)

B. Partners with Christ in service:

God is faithful, by whom ye were called unto the fellowship of his Son Jesus Christ our Lord. (1 Cor. 1:9)

(1) Workers together with God:

For we are labourers together with God: ye are God's husbandry, ye are God's building. (1 Cor. 3:9)

We then, as workers together with him, beseech you also that ye receive not the grace of God in vain. (2 Cor. 6:1)

(2) Ministers of the New Covenant:

Who also hath made us able ministers of the new testament; not of the letter, but of the spirit: for the letter killeth, but the spirit giveth life. (2 Cor. 3:6)

(3) Ambassadors:

Now then we are ambassadors for Christ, as though God did beseech you by us: we pray you in Christ's stead, be ye reconciled to God. (2 Cor. 5:20)

(4) Living epistles:

> Forasmuch as ye are manifestly declared to
> be the epistle of Christ ministered by us,
> written not with ink, but with the Spirit of
> the living God; not in tables of stone, but
> in fleshy tables of the heart. (2 Cor. 3:3)

26. Believers are recipients of eternal life:

> That whosoever believeth in him should not
> perish, but have eternal life. (John 3:15)

> And I give unto them eternal life; and they shall
> never perish, neither shall any man pluck them
> out of my hand. (John 10:28)

> But these are written, that ye might believe that Jesus
> is the Christ, the Son of God; and that believing ye
> might have life through his name. (John 20:31)

> And this is the record, that God hath given to
> us eternal life, and this life is in his Son. He that
> hath the Son hath life; and he that hath not the
> Son of God hath not life. (1 John 5:11–12)

27. The believer is created a new spiritual species:

> Therefore if any man be in Christ, he is a new
> creature: old things are passed away; behold, all
> things are become new. (2 Cor. 5:17)

28. The believer is a light in the Lord (part of the angelic conflict):

> For ye were sometimes darkness, but now are ye light
> in the Lord: walk as children of light. "Eph. 5:8"

> But ye, brethren, are not in darkness, that that day should overtake you as a thief. (1. Thess. 5:4)

29. The believer is united with the Father, Son, and Holy Spirit We are:

    A. In God:

> Paul, and Silvanus, and Timotheus, unto the church of the Thessalonians which is in God the Father and in the Lord Jesus Christ: Grace be unto you, and peace, from God our Father, and the Lord Jesus Christ. cf., "God in you." (1 Thess. 1:1)

> One God and Father of all, who is above all, and through all, and in you all. (Eph. 4:6)

    B. In Christ:

> At that day ye shall know that I am in my Father, and ye in me, and I in you. cf., "Christ in you". (John 14:20)

> To whom God would make known what is the riches of the glory of this mystery among the Gentiles; which is Christ in you, the hope of glory. (Col. 1:27)

      (1) A member in His Body:

> For by one Spirit are we all baptized into one body, whether we be Jews or Gentiles, whether we be bond or free; and have been all made to drink into one Spirit. (1 Cor. 12:13)

(2) A branch in the Vine:

> I am the vine, ye are the branches: He
> that abideth in me, and I in him, the same
> bringeth forth much fruit: for without me
> ye can do nothing. (John 15:5)

(3) A stone in the Building:

> In whom all the building fitly framed
> together groweth unto an holy temple in
> the Lord: In whom ye also are builded
> together for an habitation of God through
> the Spirit. (Eph. 2:21–22)

> Ye also, as lively stones, are built up a
> spiritual house, an holy priesthood, to offer
> up spiritual sacrifices, acceptable to God by
> Jesus Christ. (1 Pet. 2:5)

(4) A sheep in the Flock:

> My sheep hear my voice, and I know them,
> and they follow me: And I give unto them
> eternal life; and they shall never perish,
> neither shall any man pluck them out of
> my hand. My Father, which gave them
> me, is greater than all; and no man is able
> to pluck them out of my Father's hand.
> (John 10:27–29)

(5) A portion of his Bride:

> Husbands, love your wives, even as Christ
> also loved the church, and gave himself for
> it; That he might sanctify and cleanse it

with the washing of water by the word, That he might present it to himself a glorious church, not having spot, or wrinkle, or any such thing; but that it should be holy and without blemish. (Eph. 5:25–27)

And in those days shall men seek death, and shall not find it; and shall desire to die, and death shall flee from them. And the shapes of the locusts were like unto horses prepared unto battle; and on their heads were as it were crowns like gold, and their faces were as the faces of men. And they had hair as the hair of women, and their teeth were as the teeth of lions. (Rev. 9:6–8)

And there came unto me one of the seven angels which had the seven vials full of the seven last plagues, and talked with me, saying, Come hither, I will shew thee the bride, the Lamb's wife... And they shall bring the glory and honour of the nations into it. (Rev. 21:9, 26)

(6) A priest of the kingdom of priests:

But ye are a chosen generation, a royal priesthood, an holy nation, a peculiar people; that ye should shew forth the praises of him who hath called you out of darkness into his marvelous light. (1 Pet. 2:9)

(7) A saint of the "new species:"

Therefore if any man be in Christ, he is a new creature: old things are passed

away; behold, all things are become new.
(2 Cor. 5:17)

C. In the Holy Spirit:

"The Spirit in you."

But ye are not in the flesh, but in the Spirit, if so
be that the Spirit of God dwell in you. Now if
any man have not the Spirit of Christ, he is none
of his. (Rom. 8:9)

30. Every believer is the recipient of the ministries of the Holy Spirit.
He is:

A. Born of the Spirit:

He that believeth on the Son hath everlasting life:
and he that believeth not the Son shall not see life;
but the wrath of God abideth on him. (John 3:36)

B. Baptized with the Spirit:

For John truly baptized with water; but ye shall
be baptized with the Holy Ghost not many days
hence. (Acts 1:5)

For by one Spirit are we all baptized into one
body, whether we be Jews or Gentiles, whether
we be bond or free; and have been all made to
drink into one Spirit. (1 Cor. 12:13)

C. In dwelt by the Spirit:

But this spake he of the Spirit, which they that
believe on him should receive: for the Holy

Ghost was not yet given; because that Jesus was not yet glorified. (John 7:39)

And hope maketh not ashamed; because the love of God is shed abroad in our hearts by the Holy Ghost which is given unto us. (Rom. 5:5)

But ye are not in the flesh, but in the Spirit, if so be that the Spirit of God dwell in you. Now if any man have not the Spirit of Christ, he is none of his. (Rom. 8:9)

Know ye not that ye are the temple of God, and that the Spirit of God dwelleth in you? (1 Cor. 3:16)

What? know ye not that your body is the temple of the Holy Ghost which is in you, which ye have of God, and ye are not your own? (1 Cor. 6:19)

And because ye are sons, God hath sent forth the Spirit of his Son into your hearts, crying, Abba, Father. (Gal. 4:6)

And he that keepeth his commandments dwelleth in him, and he in him. And hereby we know that he abideth in us, by the Spirit which he hath given us. (1 John 3:24)

D. Sealed by the Spirit:

Who hath also sealed us, and given the earnest of the Spirit in our hearts. (2 Cor. 1.22)

And grieve not the holy Spirit of God, whereby ye are sealed unto the day of redemption. (Eph. 4:30)

E. Given spiritual gifts:

But all these worketh that one and the selfsame Spirit, dividing to every man severally as he will… Now ye are the body of Christ, and members in particular. And God hath set some in the church, first apostles, secondarily prophets, thirdly teachers, after that miracles, then gifts of healings, helps, governments, diversities of tongues. Are all apostles? are all prophets? are all teachers? are all workers of miracles? Have all the gifts of healing? do all speak with tongues? do all interpret? But covet earnestly the best gifts: and yet shew I unto you a more excellent way. (1 Cor. 12:11, 27–31)

Though I speak with the tongues of men and of angels, and have not charity, I am become as sounding brass, or a tinkling cymbal. And though I have the gift of prophecy, and understand all mysteries, and all knowledge; and though I have all faith, so that I could remove mountains, and have not charity, I am nothing. (1 Cor. 13:1–2)

31. The believer is glorified:

Moreover whom he did predestinate, them he also called: and whom he called, them he also justified: and whom he justified, them he also glorified. (Rom. 8:30)

32. The believer is complete in Christ:

> And ye are complete in him, which is the head of all principality and power. (Col. 2:10)

33. The believer is possessor of every spiritual blessing granted in eternity past:

> Blessed be the God and Father of our Lord Jesus Christ, who hath blessed us with all spiritual blessings in heavenly places in Christ. (Eph. 1:3)

34. The believer receives a human spirit (the basis of the grace apparatus for perception, along with the Holy Spirit):

> The Spirit itself beareth witness with our spirit, that we are the children of God. (Rom. 8:16)

> Now we have received, not the spirit of the world, but the spirit which is of God; that we might know the things that are freely given to us of God. Which things also we speak, not in the words which man's wisdom teacheth, but which the Holy Ghost teacheth; comparing spiritual things with spiritual. (1 Cor. 2:12–13)

> And the very God of peace sanctify you wholly; and I pray God your whole spirit and soul and body be preserved blameless unto the coming of our Lord Jesus Christ. (1 Thess. 5:23)

35. The believer has all scar tissue removed from the soul:

> I, even I, am he that blotteth out thy transgressions for mine own sake, and will not remember thy sins. (Isa. 43:25)

I have blotted out, as a thick cloud, thy transgressions, and, as a cloud, thy sins: return unto me; for I have redeemed thee. (Isa. 44:22)

36. The believer is the recipient of efficacious grace:

In whom ye also trusted, after that ye heard the word of truth, the gospel of your salvation: in whom also after that ye believed, ye were sealed with that holy Spirit of promise. (Eph. 1:13)

37. The believer is 'guaranteed a resurrection body forever:

Jesus said unto her, I am the resurrection, and the life: he that believeth in me, though he were dead, yet shall he live. (John 11:25)

38. The believer is the beneficiary of unlimited atonement:

For the love of Christ constraineth us; because we thus judge, that if one died for all, then were all dead: And that he died for all, that they which live should not henceforth live unto themselves, but unto him which died for them, and rose again... To wit, that God was in Christ, reconciling the world unto himself, not imputing their trespasses unto them; and hath committed unto us the word of reconciliation. (2 Con. 5:14–15, 19)

Who gave himself a ransom for all, to be testified in due time. (1 Tim. 2:6)

For therefore we both labour and suffer reproach, because we trust in the living God, who is the Saviour of all men, specially of those that believe. (1 Tim. 4:10)

For the grace of God that bringeth salvation hath appeared to all men. (Titus 2:11)

But we see Jesus, who was made a little lower than the angels for the suffering of death, crowned with glory and honour; that he by the grace of God should taste death for every man. (Heb. 2:9)

But there were false prophets also among the people, even as there shall be false teachers among you, who privily shall bring in damnable heresies, even denying the Lord that bought them, and bring upon themselves swift destruction. (2 Pet. 2:1)

And he is the propitiation for our sins: and not for ours only, but also for the sins of the whole world. (1 John 2:2)

39. The believer has equal privilege and equal opportunity under election and predestination.

40. Problem-solving devices are available to every believer. They are:

    A. Rebound:

    If we confess our sins, he is faithful and just to forgive us our sins, and to cleanse us from all unrighteousness. (1 John 1:9)

    B. Filling of the Holy Spirit:

    And be not drunk with wine, wherein is excess; but be filled with the Spirit. (Eph. 5:18)

C. Faith-rest drill:

Let us therefore fear, lest, a promise being left us of entering into his rest, any of you should seem to come short of it. (Heb. 4:1)

And every priest standeth daily ministering and offering oftentimes the same sacrifices, which can never take away sins. (Heb. 10–11)

D. Grace orientation:

But he giveth more grace. Wherefore he saith, God resisteth the proud, but giveth grace unto the humble. (James 4:6).

E. Doctrinal orientation:

And be not conformed to this world: but be ye transformed by the renewing of your mind, that ye may prove what is that good, and acceptable, and perfect, will of God. (Rom. 12:2)

F. Personal sense of destiny:

For to me to live is Christ, and to die is gain. (Phil. 1:21)

G. Personal love for God:

And thou shalt love the LORD thy God with all thine heart, and with all thy soul, and with all thy might. (Deut. 6:5)

Whom having not seen, ye love; in whom, though now ye see him not, yet believing, ye rejoice with joy unspeakable and full of glory: (1 Pet. 1:8)

H. Impersonal love for all mankind:

If ye fulfil the royal law according to the scripture, Thou shalt love thy neighbour as thyself, ye do well. (James 2:8)

I. Sharing the happiness of God:

These things have I spoken unto you, that my joy might remain in you, and that your joy might be full. (John 15:11)

J. Occupation with Christ:

And to know the love of Christ, which passeth knowledge, that ye might be filled with all the fullness of God. (Eph. 3:19)

The Coming of Someone Cares
A poem by Sis. Halima

The coming of someone cares
It's the creator who rules our affairs,
But you will see deep inside
That you are a part of this tribe
When dedication, commitment is there.
You will see that our task is truly great
But it's all right, it's never too late.
To commit oneself to another soul
Is the highest achievement and goal.
To give to another a helping hand
Is our creator's ultimate divine plan.
So we will run our race to the very end
Gathering people that have love within.
Gathering people that truly understand
Someone cares is the image of the divine plan.
Letting all who will listen truly know
That they are "divine, physical" and capable.
They are the 'keys to their brother's victory
By showing him love, commitment and unity.
By letting him know that he's never alone
Just let him know you are as close, as his telephone.
Just let him know you understand his affairs
But you're just here because someone cares.

Humble yourselves therefore under the mighty
hand of God, that he may exalt you in due time:
Casting all your care upon Him;
for he careth for you.
—2 Pet. 5:6, 7

Out of the Dust of Africa

In the mythopoeic world of the earliest biblical authors, it was believed that in the beginning man was formed "from the dust of the earth;" This very "dust" was envisioned as the soil of Africa. Accordingly, generic man was African/Edenic; generic man in a word *was black* by modern classifications of racial typologies. Whether you interpret Adam to have been an individual or a nation of people, it is clear that there was one Father (God) and one Mother (earth). The earth was of Africa/Eden.

"And the lord God formed man of the dust of the ground, and breathed into his nostrils the breath of life; and man became a living soul" *(Gen. 2:7)*.

8

This Is a Dedication to the Black Man and Woman

The Original People
A poem by Sis. Halima

Do you know who are the original people
Some people say they do
They say when Moses crossed the sea
His eyes were really blue
Do you know who are the original people
Now tell me, were they right
If you said Abraham, Isaac and Jacob
Were black then you are right
Did you know we were scattered
All through this big vast land
It's God who said He'll let us return
By His great powerful hand
Did you know that our forefathers
Were warriors kings and queens
They were masters at the things they did
And their studies had such meanings
Did you know that King David
Was the king and a black man
If you look deep inside yourself
You'll see his motherland
And most of all our Lord Jesus
His feet was brown like bronze
His hair was wool like a wild sheep's coat
And his countenance they did shine
No we didn't know that our people
Were the greatest in all their land
They built they sculpt they did all things
And mostly with their hands
Their monuments are here today
The pyramids they stand tall
They left us a gift of memories
So we'll know we'll never fall
No we didn't know the first scientist

Was the color of our skin
Even doctors and lawyers and engineers
Mathematicians and businessmen
No we didn't know that all medicine
Came from deep from the earth within
But our people had long discovered it
I tell you we are great women and men

I am black, but comely, O ye daughters
of Jerusalem, as the tents of Kedar,
as the curtains of Solomon.
—Song of Solomon 1:5

For too long in the history of Western civilization, persons of African descent have been stereotyped in negative ways, which have caused them to question not only their own identity but also their part in God's plan of salvation.

It is clear from studying the Scriptures that God has always separated those to whom he gave special blessings from others to whom he did not. Adam was created in the image of God and was put in a special place (the garden). The blessing of Adam passed to his descendants, who at that ancient time were reckoned only through the male line.

The original blessing that God gave to Adam was also given to Abel, not because he was a male, but because of his righteousness and ability to do what was pleasing to God (Gen. 4:1–4). The same blessing was accordingly received by Seth. In the Hebrew Bible, Set is recast as righteous in the image of his father, Noah, and as such God's blessing proceeds thenceforward nine generations to Noah, who found favor with God and was separated from the wickedness around him. These men were Sons of God, and as such received special treatment from their Father. This special blessing was passed on to the Afro-Asiatic Hebrew patriarch Abraham because, again, he separated himself from the people around him in order that he might be able to serve God in righteousness.

This blessing has yet to be fully manifested to the world because the African/Edenic man, through whom it was to come, has failed to fulfill his commission. The descendants of Abraham, Isaac, and Jacob African/Edenites the original people of God, have been chastised time after time for disobedience to their God and were driven out of their land to the four corners of the earth.

The return of diverse races of people, including those of African descent to the Holy Land, signals the manifestation of that special blessing to the world. The Bible can therefore be viewed as a testament to the cycle of chastisement and redemption and of the ultimate purpose of the Holy One of Israel. The Bible is, in short, a drama of the history of salvation in which black people play an important part.

The Diversity of the Black Religious Experience

In its broadest application, the black religious experience extends well beyond the parameters of the African American religious experience. The connotative sense of the black religious experience is simply the religion of those persons whose parentage, self-understanding, and/or physical features fall within the black (Negroid/African) race. There is an astonishing diversity of religious beliefs and practices in the history of the world's black people. This religious experience includes the religions of ancient Africa (Cush, Punt, and to a great extent ancient Egypt), as well as black adaptations of Hebraic, Jewish, Christian, and Islamic beliefs and rituals. We could also mention traditional African religions and numerous derivatives found in the black diaspora: Candomble (Brazil), Garifuna (Honduras), Shango (Trinidad), and Vodun (Haiti).

Despite this variety, the black religious experience also has denotative coherence that distinguishes it from the religious experience of other racial groups. On the one hand, the black religious experience typically considers the supernatural as a mere extension of the natural order. It seeks harmony with (not dominance over) nature, reveres ancestors, rejoices in rhythm, and takes both spirituality and the afterlife seriously. On the other hand, the impact of slavery, colonialism, and racism in the oppression of black people further clarifies the black religious experience as a designation for African Americans, especially those who represent the tradition of the black church in the United States.

What Is the Bible?

The most published book in the world is an historical record of the relationship between a particular people and a "particular God," and how the specialness of that relationship has affected the entire world. The origin of this people has been shrouded in the mysteries of the various versions and translations of the Bible (especially the King James Version) for many years.

This was due, in part, to the misinterpretations of those who rendered the original translations from Hebrew and Greek into Latin, English, and other languages. However, a large portion of the confusion stems from deliberate Eurocentric attempts to conceal what today would be called the racial and/or ethnic identity of the people of the Bible.

Today, popular Christianity too easily assumes that modern ideas about race are traceable to the Bible or that there is not a significant Black presence in the Bible Centuries of European and Euro-American scholarship along with a "save the heathen Blacks" missionary approach to Africans have created these impressions.

Despite all the evidence that indicates a manifest black biblical presence, Eurocentric church officials and scholars have tended to deny or minimize the fact that black people are in any way part of the Bible itself, a tendency that has had grave consequences for persons of African descent. Modern biblical scholarship is just beginning to overcome centuries of tragic biases against Blacks and their biblical heritage. As astonishing as it seems, most of the prestigious academies and universities of Europe and America have ridiculed the idea that Blacks have any substantive history.

The Struggle to Be Recognized

This discrimination has been long-lived. In the period between the fourth century and the Enlightenment of the seventeenth and eighteenth centuries, Europe recast the entire Bible into a saga of European people. And their interpretations have been accepted as fact by the Western world. The result has been the creation of a world in which too many Blacks themselves have become uncomfortable with images of biblical characters as Blacks.

This effort to fully recognize the black presence in the Bible is not new. For more than a century, despite their exclusion from centers of theological education, leaders in the black church have rejected the erroneous view that they were the progeny of the "accursed" Ham. A case in point is Daniel P. Seaton, DO, MD, a prominent leader in the

African Methodist Episcopal Church, who wrote in 1895 display-ing considerable knowledge about the Bible, the location of ancient religious sites, and the significance of many biblical characters. In fact, he made several field trips to Palestine. In his major work, a volume of 443 pages of text, notes, maps, and illustrations, he pro-vides extensive descriptions of tombs, villages, and other ancient sites which he visited. Regarding Ham and his descendants, Seaton offers the following:

Because these Hamites were an important people, attempts have been made to rob them of their proper place in the catalogue of the races. The Bible tells us plainly that the Phoenicians were descen-dants of Canaan, the son of Ham, and anyone who will take the time to read the Bible account of their lineage must concede the fact.

It is noteworthy that Seaton's study displays a profound aware-ness of racism among the "bona fide" Bible scholars of his day. Nevertheless, as much as we may applaud Dr. Seaton's constructive intent, clearly he could have benefited greatly from systematic histor-ical critical engagement with the biblical text in its original languages.

Recently, in America and in Africa, there has developed a pro-liferation of books and pamphlets, which represent a resurgence of what may now be called Afrocentric approaches to the Bible. Caution, however, is advised, for all students of the Bible must avoid the tendency of taking the sons of Noah-Shem ("Mongoloid"), Ham ("Negroid"), and Japheth ("Caucasian") as representing three differ-ent "races." However, this is the traditional approach of European missionaries and others who seized the opportunity thereby to des-ignate Ham as the father of Blacks, who were allegedly cursed in Genesis 9:18–29. Any reference book appearing on the subject of "Blacks in the Bible" must be held suspect, if its author tries to argue that Blacks constitute the "Hamitic" line only.

The Mythical Curse of Ham

The "curse of Ham" is a post-biblical myth. In fact, the sons of Noah-Shem, Ham, and Japheth-do not represent three different races. (It is an absurdity of no small order to claim that Noah and his wife could produce offspring that would constitute three distinct racial types!) In Genesis 9:18–29, Ham is not the recipient of a curse. The text explicitly says, "Let Canaan be cursed."

Furthermore, Ham does not mean "black" in Hebrew; it translates literally as "hot" or "heated." It does not make sense to say, logically or scientifically, that within the ten generations from Adam to Noah (and without the introduction of any outside factors), a genetic change took place which allowed one man (Noah) and his one wife (of the same race as himself) to produce children who were racially different! This is the logic many would have the modern reader believe.

Africa, the Garden of Eden
Historical Evidence

We must be prepared to bring order and clarity to the confusion, truth to the lie, and light to the darkness about ancient biblical truths. Our first task is to use biblical evidence, supportive academic references, and common sense to show that the ancestral home of man (Adam), humanity's common ancestor, was in Africa, the land associated with the beginnings of Eden in the Bible. Readers today must understand that in biblical times "Africa" included much of what European maps have come to call the "Middle East." Remember, the name Africa is actually of Latin origin and was imposed on that great continent by European explorers.

Three simple facts must be placed at the forefront of this discussion.

First, we must consider the maps of ancient biblical lands. In the Bible, there is not one single mentioning of either England or Germany; by contrast, however, countries in Africa are mentioned again and again. The Old Testament alone cites Ethiopia over forty times and Egypt over one hundred times. Many biblical and extra-biblical ancient sources mention Egypt and Ethiopia together, almost interchangeably.

Second, the Bible provides extensive evidence that the earliest people were located in Africa. The Garden of Eden account, found in Genesis 2:8–14, indicates that the first two rivers of Eden were in ancient Cush, the term that the Greeks would later transpose as "Aithlops," or Ethiopia, meaning literally "burnt face people." Genesis 2:11–12 connects the Pishon River with Havilah, a direct descendant of Cush (Gen. 10:7). The Gihon River is cited in Genesis 2:13 as the second river in Eden surrounding the whole land of Cush/Ethiopia. Clearly, wherever else "Eden" extended, its beginning was within the continent of Africa.

Third, the ancient land of Canaan was but an extension of the African land mass. In biblical times, African people frequently migrated from the continent proper through Canaan/Palestine to the east toward what was then included as Asia, namely the "Fertile Crescent," or the Tigris and Euphrates rivers of ancient Mesopotamia. This fact helps us to appreciate the term Afro-Asiatic as correctly identifying the mixed stock of people who populated the ancient Near East. Although Europeans (Greeks and Romans) began to feature in the more recent biblical narratives, the fact remains that the earliest biblical people, by modern Western standards of racial types, would have to be classified as Blacks: they were of African descent and possessed African physical features.

Color Significance and Leprosy

> And the LORD said furthermore unto him, (Moses) Put now thine hand into thy bosom. And he put his hand into his bosom: and when he took it out, behold, his hand was leprous as snow. And he said, Put thine hand into thy bosom again. And he put his hand into his bosom again; and plucked it out of his bosom, and, behold, it was turned again as his other flesh. And it shall come to pass, if they will not believe thee, neither hearken to the voice of the first sign, that they will believe the voice of the latter sign. (Exod. 4:6–8)

Moses was born in the African region of Egypt as a Hebrew and was a descendant of Abraham. While being in dialogue with God, Moses was shown an outstanding sign of God's power. By placing his hand in his bosom, it became "leprous as snow." Then upon following the same procedure the second time it "turned again as his other flesh." This other flesh without a doubt was black flesh, for leprosy had an outstanding effect upon the flesh of black people. The predominant and characteristic form of leprosy in the Old Testament is a white variety covering the entire body or a large part of its surface. Such were the cases of Moses, Miriam, Naaman, and Gehazi (Exod. 4:6; Num. 12:10; 2 Kings 5:1, 27). This act of turning black flesh white and then black again was truly a miracle.

The Vulgate and the modern Bible say that Moses's hand was "leprous as snow," but the Septuagint Bible, which is the oldest translation, dating to about 250 BC, says that Moses's hand "became as snow," and that when he placed it in his bosom the second time, "it was restored to the complexion of the other flesh" (Exod. 4:6). Here is the clearest possible inference that the miracle lay in turning black skin white, and then changing it to black again.

Never Forget
A poem by Sis. Halima

Black man don't you ever forget,
How our people crossed over on those devil ships
How they came to this land that was free,
But the natives were conquered they lost victory
How they worked as a slave night and day.
Then they built America and paved the way.
Black woman don't you ever forget,
How you were nurse for another,
Couldn't even be mother
For the ones that were of your own set.
How they took you for a prize.
And looked you deep in your eyes.
And said your mine and don't you forget.
Black children don't you ever forget,
That you're our proof we'll survive,
When we look deep in your eyes,
We see that were not conquered yet.
We see our future lives on,
In each black baby that's born.
Our kings and Queens just haven't conquered yet
So black people let us never forget,
That our warrior minds have not been snuffed
by time,
That our conquering being is checking out what
we're seeing,
That our children of old are crying out to the bold,
To stand up it's time to receive

And the LORD shall bring thee into Egypt again with
ships, by the way whereof I spake unto thee,
Thou shalt see it no more again: and there ye shall be sold
unto your enemies for bondmen and bondwomen,
and no man shall buy you.
—Deuteronomy 28:68

What Happen to Our People!

1. And it shall come to pass, if thou shalt hearken diligently unto the voice of the LORD thy God, to observe and to do all his commandments which I command thee this day, that the LORD thy God will set thee on high above all nations of the earth.

2. And all these blessings shall come on thee, and overtake thee, if thou shalt hearken unto the voice of the LORD thy God.

3. Blessed shalt thou be in the city, and blessed shalt thou be in the field.

4. Blessed shall be the fruit of thy body, and the fruit of thy ground, and the fruit of thy cattle, the increase of thy kine, and the flocks of thy sheep.

5. Blessed shall be thy basket and thy store.

6. Blessed shalt thou be when thou comest in, and blessed shalt thou be when thou goest out.

7. The LORD shall cause thine enemies that rise up against thee to be smitten before thy face: they shall come out against thee one way, and flee before thee seven ways.

8. The LORD shall command the blessing upon thee in thy storehouses, and in all that thou settest thine hand unto; and he shall bless thee in the land which the LORD thy God giveth thee.

9. The LORD shall establish thee a holy people unto himself, as he hath sworn unto thee, if thou shalt keep the commandments of the LORD thy God, and walk in his ways.

10. And all people of the earth shall see that thou art called by the name of the LORD; and they shall be afraid of thee.

11. And the LORD shall make thee plenteous in goods, in the fruit of thy body, and in the fruit of thy cattle, and in the fruit of thy ground, in the land which the LORD sware unto thy fathers to give thee.

12. The LORD shall open unto thee his good treasure, the heaven to give the rain unto thy land in his season, and to

bless all the work of thine hand: and thou shalt lend unto many nations, and thou shalt not borrow.

13. And the LORD shall make thee the head, and not the tail; and thou shalt be above only, and thou shalt not be beneath; if that thou hearken unto the commandments of the LORD thy God, which I command thee this day, to observe and to do them:

14. And thou shalt not go aside from any of the words which I command thee this day, to the right hand, or to the left, to go after other gods to serve them.

15. But it shall come to pass, if thou wilt not hearken unto the voice of the LORD thy God, to observe to do all his commandments and his statutes which I command thee this day; that all these curses shall come upon thee, and overtake thee.

16. Cursed shalt thou be in the city, and cursed shalt thou be in the field.

17. Cursed shall be thy basket and thy store.

18. Cursed shall be the fruit of thy body, and the fruit of thy land, the increase of thy kine, and the flocks of thy sheep.

19. Cursed shalt thou be when thou comest in, and cursed shalt thou be when thou goest out.

20. The LORD shall send upon thee cursing, vexation, and rebuke, in all that thou settest thine hand unto for to do, until thou be destroyed, and until thou perish quickly; because of the wicked- ness of thy doings, whereby thou hast forsaken me.

21. The LORD shall make the pestilence cleave unto thee, until he have consumed thee from off the land, whither thou goest to possess it.

22. The LORD shall smite thee with a consumption, and with a fever, and with an inflammation, and with an extreme burning, and with the sword, and with blasting, and with mildew; and they shall pursue thee until thou perish.

23. And thy heaven that is over thy head shall be brass, and the earth that is under thee shall be iron.

24. The LORD shall make the rain of thy land powder and dust: from heaven shall it come down upon thee, until thou be destroyed.

25. The LORD shall cause thee to be smitten before thine enemies: thou shalt go out one way against them, and flee seven ways before them: and shalt be removed into all the kingdoms of the earth.

26. And thy carcass shall be meat unto all fowls of the air, and unto the beasts of the earth, and no man shall fray them away.

27. The LORD will smite thee with the botch of Egypt, and with the emerods, and with the scab, and with the itch, whereof thou canst not be healed.

28. The LORD shall smite thee with madness, and blindness, and astonishment of heart.

29. And thou shalt grope at noonday, as the blind gropeth in darkness, and thou shalt not prosper in thy ways: and thou shalt be only oppressed and spoiled evermore, and no man shall save thee.

30. Thou shalt betroth a wife, and another man shall lie with her: thou shalt build an house, and thou shalt not dwell therein: thou shalt plant a vineyard, and shalt not gather the grapes thereof.

31. Thine ox shall be slain before thine eyes, and thou shalt not eat thereof: thine ass shall be violently taken away from before thy face, and shall not be restored to thee: thy sheep shall be given unto thine enemies, and thou shalt have none to rescue them.

32. Thy sons and thy daughters shall be given unto another people, and thine eyes shall look, and fail with longing for them all the day long; and there shall be no might in thine hand.

33. The fruit of thy land, and all thy labours, shall a nation which thou knowest not eat up; and thou shalt be only oppressed and crushed alway.

34. So that thou shalt be mad for the sight of thine eyes which thou shalt see.

35. The LORD shall smite thee in the knees, and in the legs, with a sore botch that cannot be healed, from the sole of thy foot unto the top of thy head.

36. The LORD shall bring thee, and thy king which thou shalt set over thee, unto a nation which neither thou nor thy fathers have known; and there shalt thou serve other gods, wood and stone.

37. And thou shalt become an astonishment, a proverb, and a byword, among all nations whither the LORD shall lead thee.

38. Thou shalt carry -much seed out into the field, and shalt gather but little in; for the locust shall consume it.

39. Thou shalt plant vineyards, and dress them, but shalt neither drink of the wine, nor gather the grapes; for the worms shall eat them.

40. Thou shalt have olive trees throughout all thy coasts, but thou shalt not anoint thyself with the oil; for thine olive shall cast his fruit.

41. Thou shalt beget sons and daughters, but thou shalt not enjoy them; for they shall go into captivity.

42. All thy trees and fruit of thy land shall the locust consume.

43. The stranger that is within thee shall get up above thee very high; and thou shalt come down very low.

44. He shall lend to thee, and thou shalt not lend to him: he shall be the head, and thou shalt be the tail.

45. Moreover all these curses shall come upon thee, and shall pursue thee, and overtake thee, till thou be destroyed; because thou hearkenest not unto the voice of the LORD thy God, to keep his commandments and his statutes which he commanded thee.

46. And they shall be upon thee for a sign and for a wonder, and upon thy seed forever.

47. Because thou servest not the LORD thy God with joyfulness, and with gladness of heart, for the abundance of all things.

48. Therefore shalt thou serve thine enemies which the LORD shall send against thee, in hunger, and in thirst, and in

nakedness, and in want of all things: and he shall put a yoke of iron upon thy neck, until he have destroyed thee.

49. The LORD shall bring a nation against thee from far, from the end of the earth, as swift as the eagle flieth; a nation whose tongue thou shalt not understand.

50. A nation of fierce countenance, which shall not regard the person of the old, nor shew favour to the young.

51. And he shall eat the fruit of thy cattle, and the fruit of thy land, until thou be destroyed: which also shall not leave thee either corn, wine, or oil, or the increase of thy kine, or flocks of thy sheep, until he have destroyed thee.

52. And he shall besiege thee in all thy gates, until thy high and fenced walls come down, wherein thou trustedst, throughout all thy land: and he shall besiege thee in all thy gates throughout all thy land, which the LORD thy God hath given thee.

53. And thou shalt eat the fruit of thine own body, the flesh of thy sons and of thy daughters, which the LORD thy God hath given thee, in the siege, and in the straitness, wherewith thine enemies shall distress thee.

54. So that the man that is tender among you, and very delicate, his eye shall be evil toward his brother, and toward the wife of his bosom, and toward the remnant of his children which he shall leave.

55. So that he will not give to any of them of the flesh of his children whom he shall eat: because he hath nothing left him in the siege, and in the straitness, wherewith thine enemies shall distress thee in all thy gates.

56. The tender and delicate woman among you, which would not adventure to set the sole of her foot upon the ground for delicateness and tenderness, her eye shall be evil toward the husband of her bosom, and toward her son, and toward her daughter.

57. And toward her young one that cometh out from between her feet, and toward her children which she shall bear: for she shall eat them for want of all things secretly in the siege and straitness, wherewith thine enemy shall distress thee in thy gates.

58. If thou wilt not observe to do all the words of this law that are written in this book, that thou mayest fear this glorious and fearful name, THE LORD THY GOD.

59. Then the LORD will make thy plagues wonderful, and the plagues of thy seed, even great plagues, and of long continuance, and sore sicknesses, and of long continuance.

60. Moreover he will bring upon thee all the diseases of Egypt, which thou wast afraid of; and they shall cleave unto thee.

61. Also every sickness, and every plague, which is not written in the book of this law, them will the LORD bring upon thee, until thou be destroyed.

62. And ye shall be left few in number, whereas ye were as the stars of heaven for multitude; because thou wouldest not obey the voice of the LORD thy God.

63. And it shall come to pass, that as the LORD rejoiced over you to do you good, and to multiply you; so the LORD will rejoice over you to destroy you, and to bring you to nought; and ye shall be plucked from off the land whither thou goest to possess it.

64. And the LORD shall scatter thee among all people, from the one end of the earth even unto the other; and there thou shalt serve other gods, which neither thou nor thy fathers have known, even wood and stone.

65. And among these nations shalt thou find no ease, neither shall the sole of thy foot have rest: but the LORD shall give thee there a trembling heart, and failing of eyes, and sorrow of mind:

66. And thy life shall hang in doubt before thee; and thou shalt fear day and night, and shalt have none assurance of thy life.

67. In the morning thou shalt say, Would God it were even! and at even thou shalt say, Would God it were morning! for the fear of thine heart wherewith thou shalt fear, and for the sight of thine eyes which thou shalt see.

68. And the LORD shall bring thee into Egypt again with ships, by the way whereof I spake unto thee, Thou shalt see it no more again: and there ye shall be sold unto your enemies for bondmen and bondwomen, and no man shall buy you.

A Prophetic Return to Egypt

In Deuteronomy 28:68, we find the prophetic statement made by God that the African Hebrews would be returned to Egypt again. But, this time, "by way of ships and there they would be sold unto their enemies for bondmen and bondwomen." It is certain that this prophecy fell upon only one people on the face of this earth, the people of Africa-the victims of the greatest, most cruel, vicious, and horrifying slave trade in the annals of history.

In their quest to escape the onslaught of destruction that came upon Jerusalem in AD 70 by the Roman General Titus, the African Hebrews fled westward and southward into northern and central Africa. This invasion of Jerusalem and the conquest of this region caused the final dispersion of all the remnants of the

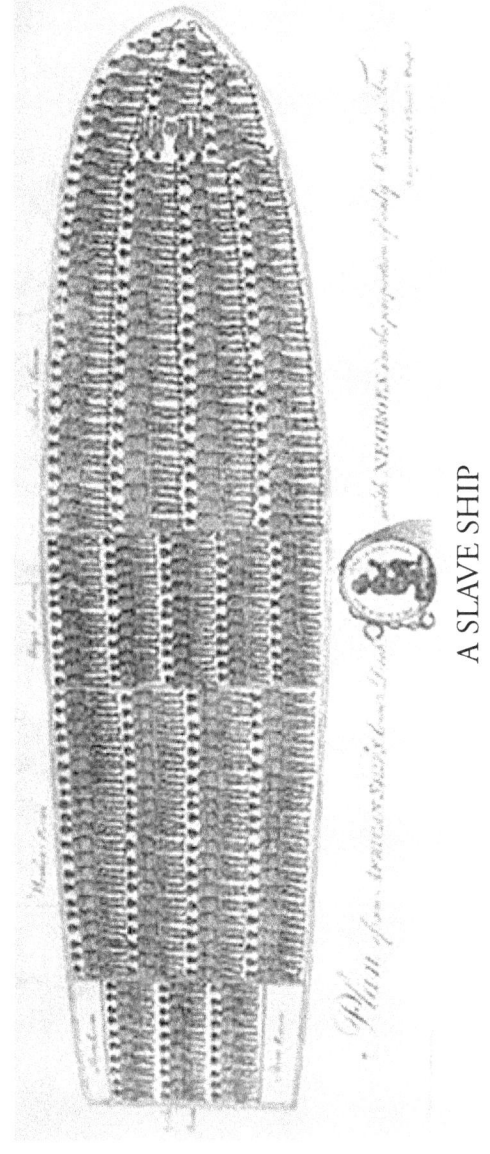

A SLAVE SHIP

black northeast African tribespeople. This flight into northern, central, and western Africa placed the African Hebrews in position for the fulfillment of the" prophecy, the great African slave trade. This brought about the final phase of chastisement and the disbursement of the people of Africa into Europe and the lands of the Americans, the "New World."

The African slaves were transported to the New World (a second Egypt) in the bottoms of slave ships, under the most inhumane conditions. These people were stretched out face-to-face in two lines, and in the space between their feet were others lying on their backs. The ships were packed to the brim. On board, the most frequent sicknesses were scurvy, dysentery, and the "pian", a skin disease. The high mortality rate led to a large number of suicides. Floors of the compartments were covered with so much mucous from the dysentery cases that the scene resembled a slaughter house.

God's prophecy upon Israel to "bring thee into Egypt again with ships" was fulfilled. Over 100 million people were either taken as captives or killed in the slave wars. About one-third of the Africans taken from their homes died on the way to the coast and at the embarkation stations, and another third died at sea, so that only one third finally survived to become the laborers in the New World.

The great captivity in the Americas not only enslaved the peoples of Africa/Eden physically, but it also served as a means used to remove all former knowledge, history, language, and culture from the minds of the slaves. A great international religious conspiracy was formulated to destroy the truth of their relationship with the true and living God.

The African/Edenic people have been the most abused, exploited, and oppressed peoples in all of history and only God can bring about their redemption and salvation. God said "no man shall buy you." No man shall intercede on the behalf of the African/Edenic people except that he is sent by God Almighty Himself to break the bonds of slavery.

The Lord Our Righteousness Will Gather the Remnant

Thus says the Lord GOD:

> When I have gathered the house of Israel from
> the peoples among whom they are scattered, and
> am hallowed in them in the sight of the Gentiles,
> then they will dwell in their own land which I
> gave to My servant Jacob. And they will dwell
> safely there, build houses, and plant vineyards;
> yes, they will dwell securely, when I execute
> judgments on all those around them who despise
> them. Then they shall know that I am the LORD
> their God. (Ezek. 28:25–26)

And I will gather the remnant of my flock out of all countries
whither I have driven them, and will bring them again to their folds;
and they shall be fruitful and increase. And I will set up shepherds
over them which shall feed them: and they shall fear no more, nor
be dismayed, neither shall they be lacking, saith the LORD. Behold,
the days come, saith the LORD, that I will raise unto David a righteous Branch, and a King shall reign and prosper, and shall execute
judgment and justice in the earth. In his days, Judah shall be saved,
and Israel shall dwell safely: and this is his name whereby he shall be
called the LORD OUR RIGHTEOUSNESS. Therefore, behold, the days
come, saith the LORD, that they shall no more say, The LORD liveth,
which brought up the children of Israel out of the land of Egypt;
But, The LORD liveth, which brought up and which led the seed of
the house of Israel out of the north country, and from all countries
whither I had driven them; and they shall dwell in their own land
(Jer. 23:3–8)

And it shall come to pass in the last days, that the mountain of
the LORD's house shall be established in the top of the mountains,
and shall be exalted above the hills; and all nations shall flow unto it.
And many people shall go and say, Come ye, and let us go up to the
mountain of the LORD, to the house of the God of Jacob; and he will

teach us of his ways, and we will walk in his paths: for out of Zion shall go forth the law, and the word of the LORD from Jerusalem. And he shall judge among the nations, and shall rebuke many people: and they shall beat their swords into plowshares, and their spears into pruning hooks: nation shall not lift up sword against nation, neither shall they learn war any more. O house of Jacob, come ye, and let us walk in the light of the LORD (Isa. 2:2–5)

Royalty Has Come
A poem by Sis. Halima

Stand up! There's a king in the room
Stand up! There's a queen in the room
Did you see them when they came through the door
They had their heads up—not to the floor
Stand up! Royalty has come
The black man and woman have won
Did you see them how they changed their minds
They started studying that was the first sign
Then they looked back in ancient times
And found out they were the first one in line
Stand up! Royalty has come
The black man and woman have won
Did you see them how they changed their names
That was the second thing: they had to be reclaimed
They wanted each and every nation to see
That every black man and woman have unity
Did you see them when they put their drugs down
That was the third thing: they did it all over town
They found out that was the key that was keeping them down
So now they're walking proud with their crowns
Stand up! Royalty has come
The black man and woman have won
Did you see them when they started reading the word
That was the fourth thing:
They're not going by what they've heard
So now black men and women have unity
That's why we stand up—because we're free
So stand up! Royalty has come
The black man and woman have won
Stand up! Royalty has come
If you're black than you have won

> *But ye are a chosen generation, a royal priesthood, a holy nation,*
> *a peculiar people; that ye should shew forth the praises of him*
> *who hath called you out of darkness into his marvelous light.*
> *—*1 Peter 2:9

Genealogy of Jesus

> Now the birth of Jesus Christ was on this wise:
> When as his mother Mary was espoused to
> Joseph, before they came together, she was found
> with child of the Holy Ghost. Then Joseph her
> husband, being a just man, and not willing to
> make her a public example, was minded to put
> her away privily. But while he thought on these
> things, behold, the angel of the Lord appeared
> unto him in a dream, saying, Joseph, thou son
> of David, fear not to take unto thee Mary thy
> wife: for that which is conceived in her is of the
> Holy Ghost. And she shall bring forth a son, and
> thou shalt call his name Jesus: for he shall save his
> people from their sins. (Matt. 1:18–21)

The genealogy of Jesus is both Hamitic and Semitic (traced through the descendants of Ham and Shem). Originally, both groups were people of color and closely associated with Africa. By modern American legal standards, anyone with a minuscule amount of African ancestry is considered Black and accordingly, this would include Jesus, even though in antiquity there were no such racial typologies or race prejudice. Matthew's inclusion of Rahab, the prostitute of Jericho who saved Joshua, is significant here. Besides underlining the fact that the Hebrew Bible provides many precedents of non-Jews or Hebrews making it possible to continue the history of salvation, the mention of Rahab here as married to Salmon the mother of Boaz connects her and eventually Jesus with the Hamitic line. Also worthy of mention is Matthew's stress upon the royal lineage of Jesus. Matthew makes frequent reference to Jesus as the Son of David (Matt.22:41–45).

The Birth of Jesus. The birth of Jesus was the source of much speculation, surprise, and polemic between Jews and Christians. Both Mary and Joseph were of typical Afro-Asiatic stock as people of color of first century Palestine; clearly, they were not Europeans as routinely pictured in Western art. In many locations in Europe and North Africa, the Madonna and Christ child are both depicted as Black. Throughout the world, many Christians of all races worshiped the Black Madonna as the original representation of "the Mother of God." This has been the case despite the fact that as early as the Byzantine Period, the Greek Orthodox

The Ancient of Days

> "I beheld till the thrones were cast down, and the Ancient of days did sit, whose garment was white as snow, and the hair of his head like the pure wool: his throne was like the fiery flame, and his wheels as burning fire" (Dan. 7:9).

This is a description of the "ancient of days," another reference to the Messiah. What is outstanding about this passage is that it reveals the African attributes of the Messiah. He is described as wearing a garment as white as snow and the hair of His head is like the pure wool: the referral to His hair being like pure wool is of particular interest and importance. This scripture also ties into the descriptive verses of the Messiah as they are written in Revelation 1:13–15: Here it is crystal clear that the physical characteristics of the Messiah are described as African.

Son of Man

> And in the midst of the seven candlesticks one like unto the Son of man, clothed with a garment down to the foot, and girt about the paps with a golden girdle. His head and his hairs were white like wool, as white as snow; and his eyes were as a flame of fire; And his feet like unto fine brass, as if they burned in a furnace; and his voice as the

sound of many waters. And he had in his right hand seven stars: and out of his mouth went a sharp two edged sword: and his countenance was as the sun shineth in his strength. (Rev. 1:13–16)

Here, John describes more fully the Old Testament reference to "the Ancient of Days" (God) in Daniel 7:9 whose hair was like "pure wool." John sees similar physical features in the Messianic figure now called "the Son of Man," whose "hairs were like white wool, as white as snow," adding that his feet were as of "fine brass." European and American white Bible translators have intentionally rendered this description in a manner to minimize the Negroid features clearly evident in the original Old Testament Hebrew and New Testament Greek texts.

The Spirit and the Bride say come…

And he saith unto me, Seal not the sayings of the prophecy of this book: for the time is at hand. He that is unjust, let him be unjust still: and he which is filthy, let him be filthy still: and he that is righteous, let him be righteous still: and he that is holy, let him be holy still. And, behold, I come quickly; and my reward is with me, to give every man according as his work shall be.

I am Alpha and Omega, the beginning and the end, the first and the last. Blessed are they that do his commandments, that they may have right to the tree of life, and may enter in through the gates into the city.

For without are dogs, and sorcerers, and whoremongers, and murderers, and idolaters, and whosoever loveth and maketh a lie.

I Jesus have sent mine angel to testify unto you these things in the churches. I am the root and the offspring of David, and the bright and morning star.

And the Spirit and the bride say, Come. And let him that heareth say, Come. And let him that is athirst come. And whosoever will, let him take the water of life freely.

For I testify unto every man that heareth the words of the prophecy of this book, if any man shall add unto these things, God shall add unto him the plagues that are written in this book:

And if any man shall take away from the words of the book of this prophecy, God shall take away his part out of the book of life, and out of the holy city, and from the things which are written in this book.

He which testifieth these things saith, Surely I come quickly. Amen. Even so, come, Lord Jesus. The grace of our Lord Jesus Christ be with you all. Amen. (Rev. 22:10–21)

The Duty of a Black Man
A poem by Sis. Halima

The duty of a black man to his mate
Is to protect encourage and dedicate
All the things he truly, truly feel
That is good
Give from his soul as no other proud
Black man would
Giving the love that only he can truly give
Showing her kindness so she can see
Her purpose to live
He'll give her gifts of life that only
He can produce
He'll give her love, devotion that will
Never let loose
He'll let her know that she is his
Bright shining star
She is his queen his queen by far

And God said, Let us make man in
our image, after our likeness:
and let them have dominion over the fish
of the sea, and over the fowl of the air,
and over the cattle, and over all the earth,
and over every creeping thing that
creepeth upon the earth.
—Genesis 1:26

It's Your Duty
A poem by Sis. Halima

The duty of a Black Woman to her man
is to love cherish and understand
it's to know exactly what he's fighting for
it's to keep him strong throughout this war
it's to give him peace and perfect harmony
it's to praise him when he has victory
it's to whisper Love always come to me
Just remind him that he is free
it's to keep him warm while he's lying down
Put a smile on his face
where there once was a frown
Give him faith, encouragement and loyalty
Dedication give him something he can really see
it's to build him up when he's fallen down
Let him know you'll be there
she'll put his feet on the ground
Let him know that he is your king of the land
He's your one and only Black Man

> *And the LORD God said, It is not good*
> *that the man should be alone;*
> *I will make him an help meet for him.*
> —Genesis 2:18

Poems of Inspiration and Words of Encouragement

By Jameselda (Sister Halima) Tinsley

© 2018

All Things through Christ
A poem by Sis. Halima

When the world just keeps on pounding
On your burdens that's already here.
When the doors you come to
Are closing before you
And your heart is filled only with fear.
When you see this world around you
Collapsing before your very eyes.
And the only thing that your ears hear
Is the suffering of human cries.

There's someone who wants me to tell you.
Through our weakness, he will be our strength.
They'll be times when we cry, we must realize
Jesus Christ our Savior has been sent.
He's been sent to take away our burdens.
He's been sent to take away our fears.
He's been sent to give us the strength to endure.
It is He that will wipe away all tears.

So if at this time you are hungry
Or if at this time you are full.
Just know in your heart it is Christ above
That will give us the strength to endure.
It is He that will show us his mercies.
When we're up or when we are down.
It is He that has stored up the gifts of God.
They await us—our own precious crowns.

I can do all things through Christ
which strengtheneth me.

(Phil. 4:13)

Christ

For God so loved the world that he gave his only begotten son that whosoever believeth in him should not perish but have everlasting life. (John 3:16)

Now in Christ Jesus you who sometimes we're far off are made near by the blood of Christ. (Eph. 2:13)

Beloved, let us love one another: for love is of God; and every one that loveth is born of God, and knoweth God. He that loveth not knoweth not God; for God is love. In this was manifested the love of God toward us, because that God sent his only begotten Son into the world, that we might live through him. Herein is love, not that we loved God, but that he loved us, and sent his Son to be the propitiation for our sins. Beloved, if God so loved us, we ought also to love one another. (1 John 4:7–11)

And immediately I was in the spirit: and, behold, a throne was set in heaven, and one sat on the throne. And he that sat was to look upon like a jasper and a sardine stone: and there was a rainbow round about the throne, in sight like unto an emerald. And round about the throne were four and twenty seats: and upon the seats I saw four and twenty elders sitting, clothed in white raiment; and they had on their heads crowns of gold. And out of the throne preceded lightnings and thunderings and voices: and there were seven lamps of fire burning before the throne, which are the seven Spirits of God. And before the throne there was a sea of glass like unto crystal: and in the midst of the throne, and round about the throne, were four beasts full of eyes before and behind. And the first beast was like a lion, and the second beast like a calf, and the third beast had a face as a man, and the fourth beast was like a flying eagle. And the four beasts had each of them six wings about him; and they were full of eyes within: and they rest not day and night, saying, Holy, holy, holy, Lord God Almighty, which was, and is, and is to come. And when those beasts give glory and honour and thanks to him that sat on the throne, who liveth for ever and ever. The four and twenty elders fall down before him that sat on the throne, and worship him that liveth for ever and ever, and cast their crowns before the throne, saying, Thou art worthy, O Lord, to receive glory and honour and power: for thou hast created all things, and for thy pleasure they are and were created. (Rev. 4:2–11)

The Family Is the Key
A poem by Sis. Halima

Commitment, Dedication, Loyalty and Trust,
Patience, Endurance; that's the family to us.
Working together, with one goal in mind,
Knowing it's the Creator,
That made this family divine.
Listening, talking, and sharing;
It's for real,
Honestly communicating the love we truly feel.
Knowing it's the family
That gives us peace of mind,
Knowing when there's one who glows,
The whole family shines.

For this cause I bow my knees unto the Father of our Lord Jesus Christ of whom the whole family in Heaven and earth is named. That He would grant you, according to the riches of His glory, to be strengthened with might by His spirit in the inner man. (Eph. 3:14–16)

Victory

God hath chosen the foolish things of the world to confound the wise; and God hath chosen the weak things of the world to confound the things which are mighty. (1Cor. 1, 27)

For the Son of man is come to save that which was lost. (Matt. 18:11)

For when we were yet without strength, in due time Christ died for the ungodly. (Rom. 5:6)

God was in Christ, reconciling the world unto himself, not imputing their trespasses unto them; and hath committed unto us the word of reconciliation. Now then we are ambassadors for Christ, as though God did beseech you by us: we pray you in Christ's stead, be ye reconciled to God. For he hath made him to be sin for us, who knew no sin; that we might be made the righteousness of God in him. (2 cor. 5:19–21)

And to the angel of the church in Philadelphia write; These things saith he that is holy, he that is true, he that hath the key of David, he that openeth, and no man shutteth; and shutteth, and no man openeth. (Rev. 3:7)

Because thou hast kept the word of my patience, I also will keep thee from the hour of temptation, which shall come upon all the world, to try them that dwell upon the earth. (Rev. 3:10)

To him that overcometh will I give to eat of the tree of life, which is in the midst of the paradise of God. (Rev. 2:7)

What a Great Reunion
A poem by Sis. Halima

What a great reunion…it will truly be,
to stand together…with our family.
To stand and know…the time has come,
The Creator has made…our family as one.
What a great reunion…everyone will rejoice,
no more tears——-—no more sorrow
we'll give praises with our voice,
We'll give honor and blessings
to the Creator above…for preserving our souls
with commitment and love
What a great reunion… I know I'll be there,
Christ paid the price, and made me his heir.
I'll see Moses and Aaron
Yes I'll see Esther too
I'll see Malcolm and Martin
You'll see me'——I'll see you
What a great reunion…our Lord has prepared,
Only those with faith…in our Lord will be there.
Only those who will hear…the roll call of his voice
but the best part of it all
is that we all have a choice.

And God shall wipe away all tears from their
eyes; and there shall be no more death,
neither sorrow, nor crying, neither
shall there be any more pain; for the
former things are passed away.
—Revelation 20:4

Thus Sayeth the Lord

And this I beheld, and, lo, a great multitude, which no man could number, of all nations, and kindreds, and people, and tongues, stood before the throne, and before the Lamb, clothed with white robes, and palms in their hands; And cried with a loud voice, saying, Salvation to our God which sitteth upon the throne, and unto the Lamb. And all the angels stood round about the throne, and about the elders and the four beasts, and fell before the throne on their faces, and worshipped God, saying, Amen: Blessing, and glory, and wisdom, and thanksgiving, and honour, and power, and might, be unto our God for ever and ever. Amen. (Rev. 7:9–12)

He that overcometh shall inherit all things; and I will be his God, and he shall be my son. (Rev. 21:7)

And I saw a new heaven and a new earth: for the first heaven and the first earth were passed away; and there was no more sea. And I John saw the holy city, new Jerusalem, coming down from God out of heaven, prepared as a bride adorned for her husband. And I heard a great voice out of heaven saying, Behold, the tabernacle of God is with men, and he will dwell with them, and they shall be his people, and God himself shall be with them, and be their God. And God shall wipe away all tears from their eyes; and there shall be no more death, neither sorrow, nor crying, neither shall there be any more pain: for the former things are passed away. (Rev. 21:1–4)

And the Spirit and the bride say, Come. And let him that heareth say, Come. And let him that is athirst come. And whosoever will, let him take the water of life freely. (Rev. 22:17)

Thanks for My Son
A poem by Sis. Halima

I thank you Lord for my son,
The one you gave to me.
I thank you Lord for my son,
He's born again and free
He knows about the sacrifice
You came to give to all
He knows that there will be many who will refuse
And they will fall.
I thank you Lord that you stepped in
When no one else was there
Letting him see his Holy Father
And that he is the one who cares
I thank you Lord that he knows now
He's not the only one
Because of your precious sacrifice
He's become an adopted son
I thank you Father for your gift
That we can receive from you
Letting us know
That there' s more precious things
The only begotten son will do
And there's one thing most of all
I like to thank you for
You have given us your son
To become our open door
But when the fullness of the time was come,
God sent forth his son, made of a woman,
Made under the law, to redeem them that were
Under the law, that we might receive
Ti-ie adoption of sons. (Gal. 4:4–5)

Father's Child

Now I say: "That the heir, as long as he is a child, differeth nothing from a servant, though he be lord of all; But is under tutors and governors until the time appointed of the father." Even so we, when we were children, were in bondage under the elements of the world: But when the fullness of the time was come, God sent forth his Son, made of a woman, made under the law, To redeem them that were under the law, that we might receive the adoption of sons. (Gal. 4:1–5)

For ye have not received the spirit of bondage again to fear; but ye have received the Spirit of adoption, whereby we cry, Abba, Father. (Rom. 8:15)

And we know that all things work together for good to them that love God, to them who are the called according to his purpose. (Rom. 8:28)

He that spared not his own Son, but delivered him up for us all, how shall he not with him also freely give us all things? (Rom. 8:32)

Taken from the Lost Books of the Bible and the Forgotten Books of Eden

On the third day, God planted the garden in the midst of the Earth on the border of the world, Eastwood, beyond which toward the sunrise and finds nothing but water that encompass the whole world and reaches unto the borders of heaven.

And to the north of the garden, there is a sea of water clear and pure to the taste like unto nothing else, so that through the clearness thereof, one may look into the depths of the Earth and when a man wash himself in it, becomes clean of the cleanness thereof and white of its whiteness, even if he were dark. And God created that sea of his own good pleasure for He knew what would come of the man He should make, so that after he had left the garden on account of his transgression, men should be born in the Earth from among whom righteousness should die, whose souls God would raise at the last day when they should return to their flesh, should bathe in that water of that sea and all of them repent of their sins.

But when God made Adam go out of the garden, He did not place him on the border of northward lest he should draw near to the sea of water and he and Eve wash themselves in it and be cleansed of their sins, forget the transgressions they had committed and be no longer reminded of it and the thought of their punishment.

Then again, as to the southern side of the garden, God was not pleased to let Adam dwell in it, because when the wind blew from the north, it would bring him, on that southern side, the delicious smell of the trees of the garden.

Wherefore God did not put Adam there least he should smell the sweet smell of those trees, forget his transgressions and find consolation for what he had done, take delight in the smell of the trees and not be cleansed of his transgressions. Again also because God is merciful and great pity and governs all things in a way he alone knows, He made our father Adam dwell in the western border of the garden because on that side the earth is very broad and God commanded him to dwell there in a cave, in a rock—the Cave of Treasures, below the garden.

But when our father Adam and Eve went out of the garden they trod the ground on their feet not knowing where they were treading and when they came to the opening of the gate of the garden and saw the broad earth spread before them and covered with stones, large and small and with sand, they feared and trembled and fell on their faces from the fear that came up on them as they were as dead because therein they had heretofore been in the garden land and because at that time they were filled with the grace and the bright nature and they had not hearts turned toward earthly things, therefore God had pity on them when He saw them falling, He had pity.

But he was wounded for our transgressions; he was bruised for our iniquities: the chastisement of our peace was upon him; and with his stripes we are healed. (Isa. 53:5)

For God So Loved the World!
A poem by Sis. Halima

For God so loved the world.
That He gave His only son.
And whosoever believes in Him.
He would save each and every one.
God knows that He's perfect.
God knows that He's just
He sent Him here upon this earth
To save every one of us.

He knew from the beginning.
There'll be some that will refuse
And the condemnation they will get
Will only make them lose.
For those of us who love Him
We know from deep within
That the purpose of His coming
Was to take away all sin.

If you have heard about the Son.
And do not understand.
Our father sent him to this world.

To. die for sinful man.
And now you have a choice to make
It's something you must do.
For when Christ died to save us
He died especially for you.

For God so loved the world, that he gave his only
begotten son that whosoever believes in him
shall not perish but have everlasting life.
　　　　　　　　　　　　　　　　—John 3:16

God Is!
A poem by Sis. Halima

God is perfect
God is just
God knows every single one of us
God is loving
He knows what is true
He sent his only son down
To die for me and you
God is righteous
He makes it plain to see
That whosoever believe in Christ
Will have eternity
God is holy
He sets us all apart
He lets us know each one is judged
By what is in his heart
God is eternal
He's been here from the start
He made the sun, the moon, the stars
And spaced each one apart
God is our Father
For those who believe in Christ
He lets us all rejoice with him
Because of Christ's sacrifice.

God is a spirit: and they that worship him
must worship him in spirit and in truth.
—John 4:24

For God So Loved the World

For God so loved the world that he gave his only begotten Son, that whosoever believeth in Him should not perish, but have everlasting life. (John 3:16)

Great and marvelous are thy works, Lord God Almighty; just and true are thy ways, thou King of saints. (Rev. 15:3)

And we have seen and do testify that the Father sent the Son to be the Saviour of the world. (1 John 4:14)

In the beginning God created the heaven and the earth. (Gen. 1:1)

He that believeth on him is not condemned: but he that believeth not is condemned already, because he hath not believed in the name of the only begotten Son of God. (John 3:18)

All the saints salute you. The grace of the Lord Jesus Christ, and the love of God, and the communion of the Holy Ghost, be with you all. Amen. (2 Cor. 13:14)

Behold the Lamb of God, which taketh away the sin of the world. (John 1:29)

For the Father judgeth no man, but hath committed all judgment unto the Son: That all men should honour the Son, even as they honour the Father. He that honoureth not the Son honoureth not the Father which hath sent him. Verily, verily, I say unto you, he that heareth my word, and believeth on Him that sent me, hath everlasting life, and shall not come into condemnation; but is passed from death unto life. (John 5:22–24)

Whosoever believeth in Him should not perish, but have eternal life. (John 3:15)

God Is Light

God is light, and in Him is no darkness at all. If we say that we have fellowship with Him, and walk in darkness, we lie, and do not the truth: But if we walk in the light, as He is in the light, we have fellowship one with another, and the blood of Jesus Christ His Son cleanseth us from all sin. If we say that we have no sin, we deceive ourselves, and the truth is not in us. If we confess our sins, he is faithful and just to forgive us our sins, and to cleanse us from all unrighteousness. If we say that we have not sinned, we make him a liar, and his word is not in us. (1 John 1:5–10)

The Word

In the beginning was the Word, and the Word was with God, and the Word was God. The same was in the beginning with God. All things were made by Him; and without Him was not anything made that was made. In Him was life; and the life was the light of men. (John 1:1–4)

Jesus said unto them, truly, truly, I say unto you, Before Abraham was, I am. (John 8:58)

I am the good shepherd: the good shepherd giveth his life for the sheep. (John 10:11)

I am the good shepherd, and know my sheep, and am known of mine. As the Father knoweth me, even so know I the Father: and I lay down my life for the sheep. (John 10:14–15)

What a Sacrifice
A poem by Sis. Halima

Oh what a sacrifice you gave to me
You gave your life so that I can be free
Oh what a sacrifice to come down on earth
You died on the cross
Especially for my rebirth
Oh what a sacrifice to be beat just for me
Took away all my sins and gave me eternity
There's no one who compares
With the life that you gave
Whosoever will come you allows to be saved
There's no money to give
For the price that you paid
Give you honor and praise
For that new life you gave
If there's some who doubts
And you do not believe
Take a look at your bible
You will see as you read
He's the One who's called Christ
The only One who can save
He took our sins on his shoulders
And his life he gave
He's the one who left all to die
For you and for me
He tells the devils depart
They have no choice but to flee
He lets us know he's the door
And there's no price to come in
He lets us see victory
And in the end, we will win

I am the door: if any man enter in,
He shall be saved,
And shall go in and out,
And find pasture.

(John 10:9)

Lord

I am the way, the truth, and the life: no man cometh unto the Father, but by me. (John 14:6)

I am the resurrection, and the life: he that believeth in me, though he were dead, yet shall he live: And whosoever liveth and believeth in me shall never die. (John 11:25–26)

Let not your heart be troubled: ye believe in God, believe also in me. In my Father's house are many mansions: if it were not so, I would have told you. I go to prepare a place for you. And if I go and prepare a place for you, I will come again, and receive you unto myself; that where I am, there ye may be also. (John 14:1–3)

Christ a Sacrifice

For there is one God, and one mediator between God and men, the man Christ Jesus; Who gave himself a ransom for all, to be testified in due time. (1 Tim. 2:5–6)

Stand fast therefore in the liberty wherewith Christ hath made us free, and be not entangled again with the yoke of bondage. (Gal. 5:1)

The Spirit of the Lord is upon me, because he hath anointed me to preach the gospel to the poor; he hath sent me to heal the brokenhearted, to preach deliverance to the captives, and recovering of sight to the blind, to set at liberty them that are bruised. To preach the acceptable year of the Lord. (Luke 4:18–19)

Let this mind be in you, which was also in Christ Jesus: Who, being in the form of God, thought it not robbery to be equal with God: But made himself of no reputation, and took upon him the form of a servant, and was made in the likeness of men: And being found in fashion as a man, he humbled himself, and became obedient unto death, even the death of the cross. (Phil. 2:5–8)

Jesus answered: Truly, truly I say unto thee, Except a man be born of water and of the Spirit, he cannot enter into the kingdom of God. That which is born of the flesh is flesh; and that which is born of the Spirit is spirit. (John 3:5–6)

But he was wounded for our transgressions; he was bruised for our iniquities: the chastisement of our peace was upon him; and with his stripes we are healed. (Isa. 53:5)

But if we walk in the light, as he is in the light, we have fellowship one with another, and the blood of Jesus Christ his Son cleanseth us from all sin. If we say that we have no sin, we deceive ourselves, and the truth is not in us. If we confess our sins, he is faithful and just to forgive us our sins, and to cleanse us from all unrighteousness. (1 John 1:7–9)

If we receive the witness of men, the witness of God is greater: for this is the witness of God which he hath testified of his Son. He that believeth on the Son of God hath the witness in himself: he that believeth not God hath made him a liar; because he believeth not the record that God gave of his Son. And this is the record that God hath given to us eternal life, and this life is in his Son. (1 John 5:9–11)

Now You Can Understand Some Of The Mysteries Of The Ages

The prophets of the Old and New Testament were miracle men indeed. They did not have access to the kind of historical information that is available today. It was not there to be used. They had nothing to compare to the mass media of today in depth, breadth, or scope. There was no internet, or daily newspapers or newspapers of any kind setting forth the day-to-day actions and decisions of national leaders, both great and small.

Nor did they have anything akin to radios and televisions to bring to the fore and to analyze national and international events as fast and as suddenly as they occurred. There were no literary men who specialized in making known and interpreting the de sign of some nations with respect to others. Their libraries were not filled with volumes by the thousands wherein people could find enough information with which to analyze everything about everybody; and upon the basis of such interpretations - predictions could never be made.

Those Old and New Testament prophets knew a great deal, but they depended largely upon God for their deeper knowledge and revelations concerning their world. Yet with unerring accuracy, the prophets predicted the rise and fall of practically all the nations and empires in their turn throughout the history of the Old and New Testament times. They predicted the downfall of every great nation and empire, whose name appears in the Old Testament except one- Rome; and St. John, the New Testament Seer of Patmos, followed the example of his Old Testament predecessors and encoded messages, predicted the fall of Rome. Unto some nations the prophets said

"Woe"; for others they said: "It shall come to pass" or "The Lord will send" or "I will punish saith the Lord."

For us it's: "For this we say unto you by the word of the Lord, that we which are alive and remain unto the coming of the Lord shall not prevent them which are asleep. For the Lord HIMSELF shall descend from heaven with a shout, with the voice of the Archangel (Michael) and with the trump of God; and the DEAD IN CHRIST shall rise first; then we which are ALIVE AND REMAIN (saints only) shall be caught up together with them in the clouds. to meet the Lord IN THE AIR, and so shall we ever be with the Lord." ~ I Thess. 4:15-77.

AND "I appointed the eighth day also that the eighth day should be the first-created after my work, and that the first seven revolve in the form of the seventh thousand. and that at the beginning of the eighth thousand there should be a time of not-counting, Endless, with neither years nor months nor weeks nor days nor hours.

And now, Enoch, all that I have told thee, all that thou hast understood, all that thou hast seen of heavenly things, all that thou hast seen on earth, and all that I have written in books by my great wisdom. all these things I have devised and created from the uppermost foundation to the lower and to the end, and there is no counsellor nor inheritor to my creations. I am self-eternal, not made with hands, and without change. My thought is my counsellor, my wisdom and my word are made and my eyes observe all things how they stand here and tremble with terror. If I turn away my face, then all things will be destroyed.

And apply thy mind Enoch and know Him who is speaking to thee and take thou the books And I give thee Samuil and Raguil, who led thee up and the books and go down to earth And tell thy sons all that I have told thee, and all that thou hast seen from the lower heaven up to my throne and all the troops.

For I created all forces and there is none that resisteth me or that does not subject himself to me. For all subject themselves to my monarchy and labour for my sole rule. Give them the books of the handwriting, and they will read them and will know me for the creator of all things and will understand how there is no other God but Me.

And let them distribute the books of thy handwriting—children to children, generation to generation, nations to nations".
~ Enoch XXXIII

PEACE & LOVE

There are many books that contemporary man has rediscovered, that were written in the past, for the world to see and learn from today. Many books that were "lost" to man and relatively newly "found" enable us to examine and study them. For example: *The Book of Enoch, The Book of Adam and Eve,* and many others. We are now blessed with the freedom to examine them for ourselves.

This book gives examples of how some of the ancient books and the Holy Bible speaks about the same topics we are concern with today and gives us the freedom and opportunity to compare, learn, rediscover, and renew the spiritual aspect of so many relevant issues in our lives, all with a touch of spiritual poems.

> "So let him who hath ears to hear, let him hear"
> (Matt. 13:9).

Those with eyes to see let us see and know the Truth.

Peace and Love

www.ingramcontent.com/pod-product-compliance
Lightning Source LLC
Chambersburg PA
CBHW051304120626
46547CB00015B/2086